Topics at the Grammar-Discourse Interface

Editors: Philippa Cook (University of Göttingen), Anke Holler (University of Göttingen), Cathrine Fabricius-Hansen (University of Oslo)

In this series:

1. Song, Sanghoun. Modeling information structure in a cross-linguistic perspective.

2. Müller, Sonja. Distribution und Interpretation von Modalpartikel-Kombinationen.

3. Bueno Holle, Juan José. Information structure in Isthmus Zapotec narrative and conversation.

ISSN: 2567-3335

Information structure in Isthmus Zapotec narrative and conversation

Juan José Bueno Holle

language
science
press

Bueno Holle, Juan José. 2019. *Information structure in Isthmus Zapotec narrative and conversation* (Topics at the Grammar-Discourse Interface 3). Berlin: Language Science Press.

This title can be downloaded at:
http://langsci-press.org/catalog/book/219
© 2019, Juan José Bueno Holle
Published under the Creative Commons Attribution 4.0 Licence (CC BY 4.0):
http://creativecommons.org/licenses/by/4.0/
ISBN: 978-3-96110-129-0 (Digital)
      978-3-96110-130-6 (Hardcover)

ISSN: 2567-3335
DOI:10.5281/zenodo.2538324
Source code available from www.github.com/langsci/219
Collaborative reading: paperhive.org/documents/remote?type=langsci&id=219

Cover and concept of design: Ulrike Harbort
Typesetting: Juan José Bueno Holle, Sebastian Nordhoff
Proofreading: Ahmet Bilal Özdemir, Eitan Grossman, George Walkden, Ivica Jeđud, Jeroen van de Weijer, Kate Bellamy, Klara Kim, Phil Duncan, Teresa Proto
Fonts: Linux Libertine, Libertinus Math, Arimo, DejaVu Sans Mono
Typesetting software: XƎLATEX

Language Science Press
Unter den Linden 6
10099 Berlin, Germany
langsci-press.org

Storage and cataloguing done by FU Berlin

Freie Universität Berlin

Contents

Acknowledgments   v

List of abbreviations used in glosses   vii

Orthographic conventions   ix

1 Introduction   1
    1.1 Motivation and objectives 1
    1.2 Ethnographic setting 4
    1.3 Previous work on the language 6
    1.4 Methods 7
        1.4.1 Corpus creation 8
        1.4.2 A discourse corpus 9
    1.5 Organization of the study 10

2 Background: the basic grammatical structures of ZAI   13
    2.1 The segmental and tonal inventory 13
        2.1.1 ZAI segmental inventory 13
        2.1.2 The tonal system 15
    2.2 The structural function of prosody in ZAI 16
        2.2.1 Tones, VQMs and stress 17
        2.2.2 Previous studies on Zapotec prosody 19
        2.2.3 Prosodic properties of intonation units in ZAI 20
        2.2.4 Prosody in ZAI information structure: some initial remarks 22
    2.3 Clause structure and constituent order correlations in ZAI . . . 23
        2.3.1 Verbal morphology 23
        2.3.2 Constituent order correlations 25
        2.3.3 Summary of constituent order correlations 33
        2.3.4 The pre-verbal position and rigidity in verb-initial syntax 35
        2.3.5 The pre-verbal position in ZAI 36
    2.4 Summary and research questions 38

Contents

**3   Preferred Argument Structure and the pragmatic status of nominal
forms in ZAI**   **41**
  3.1 Preferred Argument Structure in ZAI 41
      3.1.1 Data and Methodology 41
      3.1.2 Evidence for PAS in ZAI 43
      3.1.3 PAS and the notion of Accessibility 48
      3.1.4 Accessibility and the introduction of new referents . . . 53
      3.1.5 Accessibility and co-reference 55
      3.1.6 LNPs and salience 57
      3.1.7 Pronouns and salience 60
      3.1.8 Episode boundaries 65
      3.1.9 Summary 67
  3.2 Nominal forms and the pragmatic status of referents 69
  3.3 Summary and conclusions 73
  4.1 Syntactic constraints on the overt versus zero alternation 75
      4.1.1 Reflexives 75
      4.1.2 Dependent clauses 76
      4.1.3 Adverbial clauses 78
  4.2 The overt versus zero alternation in a Pear Story monologue . . 79
  4.3 The overt versus zero form in conversation 82
  4.4 Summary and conclusions 85

5   Focus structures in ZAI   **87**
  5.1 Focus structure 88
      5.1.1 Predicate focus 88
      5.1.2 Sentence focus 92
      5.1.3 Argument focus 93
      5.1.4 The use of NGA in argument focus 96
      5.1.5 Van Valin's (1999) typology of focus structure 100
  5.2 Focus structures in discourse: predicate focus plus argument focus 103
  5.3 Summary and conclusions 107

6   Topic relations in ZAI   **109**
  6.1 Topic constructions 109
      6.1.1 Presentational constructions 110
      6.1.2 Topic-comment 111
      6.1.3 Identificational constructions 112
      6.1.4 Topicalization 115
      6.1.5 Detached or LA-marked constructions 117

6.2   Topic relations and the LA particle in discourse   118

      6.2.1   Left-detachment constructions   121

      6.2.2   Yes/no questions   122

6.3   Summary and conclusions   125

7   Conclusions and avenues for further research   **127**

7.1   Nominal forms and cognitive status   128

7.2   Topic and focus constructions   129

7.3   The LA discourse particle   131

Appendix A   **133**

Appendix B   **143**

References   **183**

Index   **193**

   Name index   193

   Language index   195

   Subject index   197

Acknowledgments

This book is a revised version of my doctoral dissertation at the University of Chicago, which I successfully defended in April 2016. As with all language documentation projects, at its core this work is a collaborative endeavor and the product of a web of valuable relationships. My deepest thanks go to the community of Juchitán, Oaxaca, and to the consultants and collaborators of this study, most especially, to my teacher Tomás Villalobos Aquino. *Diuxquixepe' lii. Cadi tutiisi rini' diidxazá.*

It is impossible for me to name everyone who made my own as well as my family's fieldwork experience in Juchitán such a rich and rewarding one. Thanks and appreciation cannot capture everything that I have learned and gained from the many relationships that have been built between many of the families in Juchitán and mine. I am forever indebted to Tomás Villalobos Aquino and Rosa López Vásquez and family for their unconditional support for me and my family from the first time we visited Juchitán. They hosted, taught, and shared with us with such generosity and openness that I only hope I one day have the words to convey to others. There is nothing more meaningful that I can take away from this project than the friendship and care that they have shown me.

I would like to highlight the contribution of Irvin Villalobos López, who worked conscientiously and consistently in reviewing, transcribing and translating many recordings. I owe a debt of gratitude to Miguel Villalobos Aquino and family. Their warm hospitality and enthusiasm for all things were infectious and a wonderful source of comfort, especially during so many months of intense heat. I cannot thank the Saynes Vásquez family enough for all of the openness and generosity they showed me and my family. I am very grateful to Na Ernestina, Ta Cecilio, and Ta Ulises and family for all of their great help and friendship, and for offering a place to make hammocks and to just be. Na Maria Reina and family shared their home and their lives with us in the most generous and happiest of ways. I wish to thank Porfirio Matus Santiago for sharing so much of his language with me and with so much enthusiasm. I am thankful to everyone at Lidxi Guendabiaani' for always welcoming me with open doors, literally. Yolanda López Gómez offered a great deal of trust and unwavering support.

Acknowledgments

I wish to thank my editor Philippa Cook and for her dedication to this series and for her strong support of this project. I am grateful to the anonymous reviewers for their close reading and insightful critique and to the anonymous proofreaders for their attention to detail. Finally, I wish to thank Sebastian Nordhoff for his precise and energetic work in getting this book to press. All remaining errors are my own.

This work was stimulated and guided by my professors at the University of Chicago. I am extremely grateful to Lenore Grenoble for her tireless support of this project from the beginning and her sustained guidance has been astute, inspirational and energizing. Amy Dahlstrom was instrumental ever since I first began to analyze the overt/zero third person pronoun alternation and the LA particle. Michael Silverstein provided much needed support, encouragement, and motivation through many enlightened and productive conversations.

The main fieldwork for this project was made possible by grants from the Endangered Languages Development Programme (ELDP), the National Science Foundation's Documenting Endangered Languages program (NSF-DEL), and the Jacobs Research Fund. A large part of the writing stage was completed during a 12-month fellowship at the Smithsonian Institution. I am especially grateful to Gabriela Pérez Báez for her generous and valuable help. I also would like to thank Mark Sicoli for his insightful comments and suggestions.

I would like to especially thank Eduardo Toledo García who made not one journey but countless journeys possible between Juchitán and Mexico City as well as across the Isthmus and within the state of Oaxaca, offering everything he could, including his car, his driving, his good humor, and his care. Patricia Bustamante Herrera and Donají Toledo Bustamante have treated me as a family member ever since I first met them. Hortencia Toledo and Vicente Orozco lovingly welcomed us into their home on so many occasions, I do not think I can remember them all.

I am extremely thankful to my parents, Javier Bueno and Nina Holle, who have supported me and my family in countless ways. The same is true for my brothers, Carlos and Francisco, who have contributed in ways that they probably do not imagine.

Finally, this work benefited greatly from the deep insight and solidarity of Nadxieli Toledo Bustamante. Paula has made the journey with us and has enriched every part of it. It is truly special to have shared our time in Juchitán together and to now be able to share this with them.

List of abbreviations used in glosses

1	first person	INTJ	interjection
2	second person	IMP	imperative
3	third person	IRR	irrealis
ANIM	animate	LA	discourse particle LA
AUG	augmentative	LOC	locative
BASE	base for enclitic pronoun	NEG	negation
CAUS	causative	NGA	discourse particle NGA
COMPL	completive	PART	participle
DEM	demonstrative	PERF	perfect
DIM	diminutive	PL	plural
DIST	distal	POSS	possessive
EMPH	emphatic	POT	potential
EXCL	exclusive	PP	preposition
FUT	future	PROG	progressive
HAB	habitual	Q	question particle
HUM	human	RECIP	reciprocal
INAN	inanimate	REL	relative
INCL	inclusive	SG	singular
INDEF	indefinite	STAT	stative

Orthographic conventions

Throughout, I use the standard written orthography of ZAI (*Alfabeto popular para la escritura del zapoteco del Istmo* 1956), which generally follows the orthographic conventions of Mexican Spanish, for example:

ch	/tʃ/
g and *gu*	/g/
hu	/w/
gü	/gw/
dx	/dʒ/
xh	/ʃ/
x*	/ʒ/

*Note, however, that *x* before voiceless consonants is pronounced [ʃ]; often used as POSS morpheme.

Although ZAI is a tonal language, tone is not marked in the ZAI orthography. I note the underlying tonal information in the gloss (the superficial tones can be straightforwardly derived from the underlying tones – although this requires more investigation (Pérez Báez, p.c.) – and use the following notation for tones:

rising (LH) tone	[^{LH}]
high (H) tone	[^{H}]
low (L) tone	unmarked
Glottalized vowels	apostrophe ['] immediately after the vowel
Laryngealized vowels	two consecutive vowels, [VV] (still within a single syllable)

1 Introduction

1.1 Motivation and objectives

Linguists have begun to uncover commonalities across the world's languages with respect to the way discourse is organized and cross-linguistic research has shown a wide range of typological phenomena associated with different components of information structure (Bernini & Schwartz 2006; Mereu 2009; Erteschik-Shir 2007). However, because the great majority of research in this area is done on well-documented, non-endangered languages, comprehensive cross-linguistic research remains difficult. This study aims to conceptualize this interaction in more precise ways by presenting the main linguistic strategies by which speakers of Isthmus Zapotec, a tonal and verb-initial language spoken in Oaxaca, Mexico, convey information. The study of discourse and information structure is scarce in tonal and verb-initial languages and extremely lacking for the great majority of Mesoamerican languages including those in the Otomanguean stock (cf. Camacho et al. 2010; Lillehaugen 2008; 2016).

Isthmus Zapotec (ISO 639 code: ZAI) is a Central Zapotec language of the Otomanguean stock spoken by approximately 50,000 speakers in and around the region of Juchitán, Oaxaca, Mexico although, increasingly, the language is under threat due to a rapid shift to Spanish. Several different attempts at a classification of the Zapotec languages have been made throughout the history of their documentation (see Smith-Stark 2003; Campbell 2017b,a for a detailed overview). Although no consensus has been reached as to which classification is the most accurate, it has become clear that the diversity of Zapotec languages is extremely rich. Nevertheless, while a considerable amount of work has been done, especially in recent years, on the documentation and description of the grammars of these languages (e.g. Avelino 2004; Beam de Azcona 2004; Sonnenschein 2005), very few studies have been devoted to analyzing naturally-occurring discourse and the way these languages are used by speakers in everyday life (cf. Castillo Hernández 2014).

More specifically, I draw on a corpus I collected through 17 months of fieldwork as well as on a relatively large body of existing documentation to present a study of *information structure*. In this, I generally follow the framework established by Lambrecht (1994) which understands information structure as the study of how the different components of sentences – intonation, morphology, and syntax – are organized with respect to each other in discourse to signal topic, focus, definiteness, and the accessibility of referents. One way to think about information structure is in terms of 'information packaging' and by considering hypotheses about the receiver's assumptions as crucial to discourse structure (Chafe 1994; Lambrecht 1994). These are the sender's hypotheses about the status of the referent of each linguistic expression, as represented in the mind of the receiver at the moment of an utterance. Thus, for studies on information structure, it is the way the information is transmitted that is critical, rather than the lexical or propositional content of a sentence, around which grammar usually centers.

Three main observations motivate this study: 1) the combination of the existing documentation and a relatively large and active speaker community offer a unique opportunity to document information structure in ZAI and to study the language as it is used by speakers in everyday life; 2) as a tonal and verb-initial language, the study of ZAI represents a chance to explore the possible combinations of tone, intonation, morphology, and verb-initial syntax that may occur in the coding of information structure, and 3) the analysis of an endangered language contributes to our theoretical understanding of information structure and informs our knowledge of language documentation practices and revitalization efforts.

These observations lead to the following four research questions:

1. What are the different morphological forms that nominal referents in ZAI can have and how are these forms used by speakers to express different types of cognitive status?

2. Since constituent order is known to have important discourse functions in many languages and since a very small percentage of the world's languages are verb-initial, how does verb-initial syntax in ZAI condition the ways that speakers formulate their discourse to satisfy their communicative goals? Are constituent order changes a possible strategy for expressing all types of topic and focus constructions or only a subset? To what extent do phonetic and intonational cues also play a role?

3. A discourse particle, LA, is employed often in ZAI discourse. What discourse functions does this particle have?

4. What is the distribution of stress and of pauses at the phrase- or discourse-
level? Are they predictable? How do stresses and pauses interact with the
tonal system of the language? How do they interact with the expression
of topic and focus structures?

I begin by reviewing the main typological characteristics of the language, including the tone system, the structural function of prosody, and constituent order, and show that the most common arrangement of constituents in ZAI is verb
followed by subject then object. Verb-initial syntax, however, is often violated as
the pre-verbal position can be the locus for important discourse functions. The
pre-verbal position is shown to interact closely with grammatical role and pragmatic status of nominals in the expression of topic and focus relations. Through
the close examination of the form, function, and distribution of ZAI nominals, I
analyze the different nominal forms used to introduce and track referents and to
mark referents as more or less accessible. I focus specifically on the distribution
and alternation of two types of third person pronominal forms, the zero form and
the overt subject enclitic form, in spontaneous narrative and conversation and
conclude that an important factor governing their use is the relative thematic
salience of the referents: the overt enclitic is used for more thematic figures and
the zero form for less thematic figures.

I then build on this discussion of nominal forms to address topic and focus
relations. I find that while sentence focus and predicate focus constructions are
consistently verb-initial, argument focus constructions may contain either pre-
verbal constituents (within the clause) or, alternatively, may be verb-initial. No
evidence is found for pitch accents directly associated with focal material.

The analysis of topic and focus relations is extended in the latter chapters by
examining data from narrative and conversational contexts where ZAI speakers
employ topic and focus constructions for specific interactional purposes. I examine a conversational strategy in which ZAI speakers use predicate focus and
argument focus successively. The combined use of predicate focus and argument
focus is analyzed as a chiastic structure in which the speaker binds two intonation units into a couplet to be interpreted together. One effect of this use is to
extend his/her speaking turn for an additional intonation unit, with the second
part, the argument focus construction, marking the end of the speaker's turn,
ceding the floor.

The work concludes with a detailed look at a multifunctional discourse particle, LA. I show that it is used in topic-promoting contexts, as well as to mark
"scene-setting topics" that have a frame-setting or delimiting function, to indicate

changes in topics or boundaries of topical units, and for contrastive topics. I conclude that LA-marked constructions should be viewed not only as a resource for marking various types of topical information, but more generally as a resource for organizing talk and interaction.

Overall, the analysis demonstrates the value of and need for information structure studies to document and analyze spontaneous and naturally-occurring discourse, particularly in understudied and endangered languages. The primary goal is to extend the analysis of the syntax-pragmatic interface beyond the notions of topic and focus to incorporate phenomena that have a function clearly linked to the structuring of discourse and interaction. To put it another way, although the direct elicitation of topic and focus constructions will be shown to be useful for understanding the range of morphological and syntactic combinations available to speakers, the close analysis of narrative and conversation offers an opportunity to connect information structure phenomena to – and find explanatory reasons in – the broader discursive and interactional contexts in which they are situated.

1.2 Ethnographic setting

ZAI is spoken by approximately 50,000 people in and around Juchitán de Zaragoza, in southern Oaxaca, Mexico. The language is under threat due to a rapid shift to Spanish which has left towns such as La Ventosa, north of Juchitán, with no children actively learning the language (Gabriela Pérez Báez, p.c.). The region of Juchitán, Oaxaca was populated by the Zapotecs approximately 200 years before Spanish contact, making ZAI one of the latest to diverge from the Central branch of the Zapotec language family (Rendón 1995). Today, with the important port of Salina Cruz only 30 km south, the city of Juchitán is a small, sprawling urban center with 100,000 residents, located on the highway and railroad routes that cross the Isthmus of Tehuantepec and create a bridge between the Gulf of Mexico and the Pacific Ocean. In a country where the great majority of indigenous languages are associated with small, rural communities, Juchitán is unusual because, while it is also home to white and mestizo elites, it has a majority ZAI-speaking population which has managed to maintain a very strong indigenous identity and culture. This is one reason why the city is home to the first independent indigenous radio station in the country, Radio Teka.

Still, for almost five centuries, Spanish has served as the language of government, of the formal job market, and of the mainstream media and, increasingly

Figure 1.1: A linguistic map of the Isthmus of Tehuantepec (based on Paul et al. 2016). Language families represented are Nahuatl (red), Mixe-Zoquean (tan), Zapotec (blue), Chontal (green), Huave (orange).

with each generation, is replacing the indigenous language.[1] Today, the impact of Spanish on ZAI is even stronger than it has ever been, especially since the expansion of the public school system and instruction in Spanish about 50 years ago. Although the percentage of ZAI-speaking residents older than 50 is quite high, the percentage of children that are growing up speaking the language is comparatively low, hovering around 50% (Augsburger 2004). So, although stable Spanish-ZAI bilingualism has been the norm for several centuries, in many areas the language shift from ZAI to Spanish is now occurring very quickly and may even complete itself within the next generation (Augsburger 2004).

Juchitán is distributed geographically into sections and, with the growing population, the city has extended beyond the original eight sections. In this growth, it is increasingly noticeable that the divisions between the sections mark patterns of language use such that these patterns roughly correlate with socio-economic differences. Although the adult population is overwhelmingly bilingual throughout the city, certain sections of the city, like the *séptima* and *cheguigo* contain the majority of the ZAI-dominant speakers. These sections also contain higher

---

[1]This is true for all or most of the indigenous languages across the country. The complex sociopolitical process that has led to this situation is the subject of Heath (1972).

concentrations of people engaged in traditional occupations, such as artisans and fishermen. In contrast, sections such as the *primera, segunda* and *tercera* are Spanish-dominant. These sections are middle-class neighborhoods and contain a wider range of occupations.[2]

One significant outcome, then, of the increasing rate of shift of the younger generation in favor of Spanish is that the range of use of ZAI is being gradually reduced to specific sections of the city as well as to certain social networks with specific socioeconomic characteristics. The reduction in the range of social situations and communicative contexts in which ZAI is employed will no doubt have a strong impact on the diversity of genres and styles in which it will come to be used in day-to-day life and, concomitantly, on the forms and functions of the spoken language itself.

1.3 Previous work on the language

The linguist Velma Pickett is responsible for a great majority of the early linguistic documentation and analysis of ZAI. Beginning her work on ZAI in the 1950's, much of Pickett's work in those years culminated in her doctoral thesis entitled *The grammatical hierarchy of Isthmus Zapotec* (Pickett 1960), which focused primarily on a syntactic analysis of the language from the perspective of tagmemic grammar developed by Kenneth Pike. Pickett continued her work on ZAI and, with the establishment of the orthographic conventions, created a dictionary (Pickett 1979) and, with Cheryl Black and Vicente Marcial Cerqueda, developed a concise speaker grammar (Pickett et al. 1998). The dictionary and grammar together give an accurate, though very general, picture of the major aspects of the ZAI lexicon, phonology, morphology and syntax. Following Pickett's work, in the 1980's Carol Mock published several very thorough articles on the lexical phonology of ZAI (Mock 1983; 1985a,b; 1988). At around the same time, Pickett co-authored an article with Stephen Marlett entitled "The syllable structure and aspect morphology of Isthmus Zapotec" (Marlett & Pickett 1987), which offers a very good description of the ZAI syllable and the complex system of aspectual prefixes.

---

[2]See Saynes-Vásquez (2002), Augsburger (2004), and McComsey (2015: Chapter 1) for a more detailed description of the socio-linguistic make-up of the city with respect to its sections. In towns such as Xadani and San Blas, which border the main urban areas of Juchitán and Tehuantepec, respectively, and supply them with much of the manual labor, the percentages of residents older than 50 and of children between five and nine years who speak (or, at least, report speaking) ZAI are significantly higher. In other Isthmus towns as well as in Tehuantepec, the governmental center of the Isthmus, these percentages are much lower. See also Toledo Bustamante (2018).

To my knowledge, only one documentation project of ZAI has been undertaken since the work of Pickett. This was done as part of the Project for the Documentation of the Languages of Meso-America (PDLMA). This project is ongoing and is primarily dedicated to the building of a lexicon (Kaufman et al. n.d.). Neither the documentation of prosody at the phrase or discourse level nor the documentation of information structure are part of that project.

Therefore, no studies on narrative discourse or information structure in ZAI have been published or even conducted. Moreover, studies on discourse are extremely lacking for the great majority of Zapotec languages as well. One significant exception to this is the work by Mark Sicoli (Sicoli 2007; 2010) on the use of tone and intonation in Lachixío Zapotec (an Eastern Zapotecan language). Other existing work on Zapotec discourse has been done by linguists affiliated with the Summer Institute of Linguistics (SIL) (Persons 1979; Long 1985; Benton 1987; 1997; Kreikebaum 1987; Riggs 1987; Ward 1987; Piper 1995; Heise 2003; Riggs & Marlett 2010). These studies have primarily descriptive goals, they tend to focus on folk and written narrative, and are concerned mostly with specific syntactic problems and analyses at the sentence or paragraph level. Virtually no attention is paid to the role of intonation or to the major components of information structure.

Because of these studies and because of the amount of knowledge already gained in the areas of phonology, morphology, lexicon, and syntax, the opportunity to document and analyze information structure in ZAI is open. The present project looks to build on this wealth of previous work. The close study of ZAI offers a unique opportunity to explore the possible combinations of prosody, morphology and verb-initial syntax that may occur in the coding of information structure. Establishing the correlations between these areas is best determined by the analysis of spontaneous discourse. At the same time, however, one of the most straightforward ways to determine the range of possible constructions is via elicitation since this methodology makes it possible to create unambiguous contexts which trigger clearly distinct topic and focus structures. In this study, I take both methodological approaches. The rationale for utilizing this combination of methodologies is discussed in the next section.

1.4 Methods

In collecting the corpus that is the basis for this study, I worked with bilingual ZAI-Spanish language consultants in Juchitán over a 17-month period to record, transcribe, annotate and translate spontaneous speech and collect elicited native speaker judgments of constructed examples. The description that follows of information structure of the language fills a crucial gap in the empirical base of knowledge about ZAI as well as Zapotec languages more broadly, and contributes important data for more general theoretical questions about language structure and use.

1.4.1 Corpus creation

During the fieldwork stage, I recorded spontaneous speech and supplemented this with data from elicitation through traditional field methodologies. The collected recordings ensure that naturally-occurring speech forms have been documented while the elicitation sessions ensure that these forms are considered with respect to a broader set of possible combinations of tone types, intonation patterns and constituent orders. In the end, the documentary corpus allows for a more complete understanding of the range of constructions that are available to ZAI speakers and how they are employed to respond to specific discourse motivations.

In this, the project adopts a "discourse-centered approach" for documentation and description (Sherzer 1987). Focusing on naturally-occurring speech makes it possible to find and analyze words and structures that may not surface when sentences from the contact language are translated into the target language.

There are several reasons for focusing this documentation project on spontaneous speech. First, in contrast to other types of spoken genres such as ritual speech or traditional folklore which often tend to be formulaic, spontaneous speech and dialogue have the advantage of being naturally-occurring while providing extensive information about information structure. Second, it offers the possibility of simultaneously documenting popular oral histories. Third, spontaneous speech is cross-linguistically under-documented. Fourth, the long scholarly tradition and extensive analysis of conversation across disciplines in the social sciences and humanities offers a solid foundation upon which linguistic analyses can be carried out as well as a potentially fruitful avenue to pursue in the dissemination of the data. In the end, by focusing on spontaneous speech, this project underlines the importance of documenting a speech genre that is meaningfully embedded in the daily social lives of the speakers.

Still, it is important to recognize that specific constructions, word or intonation contours of interest might occur only very rarely in running speech, which makes it impractical to rely solely on free narrative and/or conversation for linguistic research of pre-determined phenomena. This is the point made by Himmelmann (2006), specifically with respect to the documentation of prosody, which a part of this project will be particularly concerned with. To this end, structured games and nonlinguistic triggers such as pictures and short video clips, were employed in elicitation sessions designed to document a range of intonational contours and constituent orders.

As noted above, Zapotecan languages are well known for being phonologically complex, containing complex interactions between tone, stress, and voice quality modifications such as glottalization and larygealization. The documentation of ZAI discourse represents a chance to document the interesting phonological and phonetic variations of the language in use and the annotation and analysis of prosodic phenomena form a central part of this project.[3]

1.4.2 A discourse corpus

The collection of material for the discourse corpus employed native speakers of ZAI as language consultants and used the following data collection methods: 1) audio and audiovisual recording of naturally occurring speech, and 2) transcription and analysis of the data. The main purpose was to begin a collection of recordings with samples of spontaneous speech, something not represented currently in any archives of the language.

The language is undergoing shift, so it was important to responsibly archive the data for future researchers and community members. Because of the hot and humid climate and because the majority of recordings were done outdoors, I used a Zoom H4n recorder and a Sony ECM-MS 957 external microphone as well as lavalier microphones. Audio recordings were made at a sampling rate of 16 bit/44 Khz. Visual recordings were made using a digital video camcorder with the same external microphones. All recordings were digitized and converted into WAV, MPEG1 and MPEG2 files to conform to Open Language Archives Community (OLAC) standards.

In-field processing of the data included the transcription, translation and annotation of the recordings with the help of native-speaker language consultants (but not the speakers themselves). The texts were represented and time-aligned to the primary data using ELAN software in a multi-tiered analysis: orthography using the Isthmus Zapotec conventions; a morpheme-by-morpheme tier with glosses in Spanish and English using transparent terminology; and free translations in both Spanish and English. All phonetic analysis was done using Praat.

Metadata for each recording is provided based on the International Standards for Language Engineering Metadata Initiative (IMDI) so as to ensure that all the

---

[3] After all, not marking prosody in transcription may result in "making something perfectly determined in speech undetermined in transcription" (Scarano 2009: 57).

relevant metadata is systematically and transparently documented. The audio and video recordings have been archived at the Endangered Languages Archive Repository (ELAR) of the Endangered Languages Documentation Programme at the School of Oriental and African Studies of the University of London. They are accompanied by transcriptions of the data and metadata files with information for each recording, all done in XML format.

The benefits of utilizing these standard documentation practices are twofold: they facilitate the proper archiving of the materials and the wider use of the resources by other people, including the community itself and they also facilitate future analyses by allowing for searches across structured annotations.

1.5 Organization of the study

This chapter discusses the motivation and objectives of the project and presents background information on Isthmus Zapotec and the speech community that is the subject of the research. It briefly describes the Isthmus Zapotec speaking population and characterizes the language's endangered status along with the socio-historical and cultural factors that shape the current linguistic situation. It surveys the existing documentation for ZAI, showing how the documentation of discourse aims to fill an important gap in the current documentation of the language. The chapter concludes with a review of the methodology employed in the data collection and creation of the corpus.

The following chapter presents a grammatical sketch of ZAI. It addresses the most relevant typological characteristics of the language, including, the phonological system, the structural function of prosody, and verb-initial syntax, focusing specifically on the role of constituent order in the expression of information structure in ZAI and showing the pre-verbal position to be the locus for a variety of discourse functions. It concludes with a summary of the main research questions that guide the rest of the study.

The main objective of Chapter 3 is to explore the relationship between, first, the form and distribution of nominals and, second, their function in discourse to introduce and track referents and to mark referents as more or less accessible. This discussion is framed in terms of the combined lens of Preferred Argument Structure and Accessibility theory. It then moves on to a discussion of the cognitive status of the various nominal forms available to ZAI speakers. Chapter 4 focuses specifically on the contrast between the overt 3SG subject enclitic and a zero form. It explores the distribution and alternation of the two third person clitics in narrative and conversation and argues that an important factor governing the use of these forms is the relative thematic salience of third-person referents.

The goal of Chapter 5 is to analyze the focus structures available in ZAI. It does so by presenting a survey of the main focus marking constructions of sentence focus, predicate focus, and argument focus (Lambrecht 1994) in order to place ZAI information structure within the typology of focus structure proposed by Van Valin (1999). The chapter explores the extent to which ZAI may be considered a more or less "rigid" verb-initial language with respect to the kinds of pragmatically-marked information that may appear in pre-verbal position. The chapter ends with the consideration of a parallel use of sequenced predicate focus and argument focus constructions in conversation.

Chapter 6 extends the analysis and the observations made in previous chapters to provide an analysis of the main topic marking strategies in ZAI, including presentational, topic-comment, and identificational constructions. The chapter ends with a discussion of the particle LA and its functions in conversation to mark pre-posed adverbial clauses and left-detached contrastive topics and, more generally, to negotiate and secure common ground between interlocutors.

The final chapter summarizes the main conclusions of the study and proposes avenues of further research.

2 Background: the basic grammatical structures of ZAI

This chapter presents a short description of the main typological characteristics of the language summarizing the aspects of ZAI grammar that are most relevant to the analysis of information structure. This description lays a foundation on which to explore the interrelationships between nominal forms, constituent orders, particles, and prosodic patterns. The chapter begins with a description of the segmental and tonal inventory and a brief explanation of the orthographic conventions used throughout. It then builds on an analysis of the ZAI tonal system in order to discuss the basic prosodic properties of the language at the phrase and discourse level, in particular the structural function of stress and pauses. The chapter then continues with an overview of ZAI verbal forms and basic clause structure. This leads into an examination of the main constituent orders in ZAI and concludes with a closer inspection of the pre-verbal position.

2.1 The segmental and tonal inventory

In this section, I offer a brief sketch of the segmental inventory and phonological system of ZAI. The information presented in this section is important for understanding the prosodic and verbal structures discussed in the remainder of the chapter.

2.1.1 ZAI segmental inventory

ZAI contains the segment inventory shown in Tables 2.1 and 2.2.

The relevant contrast between consonants with the same place of articulation has traditionally been referred to as a fortis-lenis contrast (Pickett 1960, Pickett et al. 1998; see also Arellanes 2009, Chávez Peón 2010 with respect to other Zapotec languages).[1] This fortis-lenis contrast parallels the voiced-voiceless distinction,

---

[1]This contrast has also been referred to as a morpho-phonological contrast between simple and geminate consonants (Swadesh 1947).

Table 2.1: ZAI consonant inventory

p			t	tʃ	k	
b			d	dʒ	g	
		f*	s	ʃ		h
			z	ʒ		
m			n	ɲ		
			n:			
			r*			
			ɾ			
			l			
			l:			
w				y		

(* = Appear only in loanwords)

where the lenis consonants are the voiced consonants and the fortis consonants are the voiceless consonants.

The five modal vowels all have glottalized and laryngealised counterparts (see Table 2.2).

Table 2.2: ZAI vowel inventory

i	iʔ	iʔi				u	uʔ	uʔu
e	eʔ	eʔe				o	oʔ	oʔo
			a	aʔ	aʔa			

(Modal, laryngealized, and glottalized vowels)

Glottalization is realized as a post-vocalic glottal stop in a stressed monosyllabic root (1a) (the prefix *ri* is a habitual marker) and, if the root is disyllabic, also simultaneously as a word-final glottal stop in pre-pause position (1b).

(1) a. *ri-nda'* [rìndàʔ] 'stinks' (cf. *ri-ndă* [rìndǎ] 'arrive')
     b. *bé'ñe'* [béʔɲèʔ] 'alligator' (cf. *beñe* [bèɲè] 'mud')

Laryngealization is realized as creaky vowel quality and a double pulse to the syllable (2a,b).

(2) a. *saa* [sà$^?$a] 'music'
     b. *na-dxĭibĭ* [nà-dʒĭ$^?$ibĭ] 'fearful'

Glottalization and laryngealization each interact closely with stress in ways that are discussed in more detail in §2.2.1.

2.1.2 The tonal system

There are three phonemic tones: high (H), rising (LH), and low (L). These tones, as they appear on monosyllabic and disyllabic morphemes, are shown in Table 2.3.[2]

Table 2.3: ZAI tonal inventory

	Monosyllabic	Disyllabic
H	*dxé*	*léxu*
	[dʒé]	[lé:xú]
	'boy'	'rabbit'
LH	*dxĭ*	*yŭzě*
	[dʒĭ]	[yŭ:zě]
	'quiet'	'livestock'
L	*ru*	*benda*
	[rù:]	[bèn:dà:]
	'cough'	'fish'

Importantly, morphemes which contain a rising (LH) tone on the final syllable carry a floating H tone. The floating H tone appears on the final syllable of these words in isolation, but floats onto the following syllable utterance-medially. Two examples of words uttered in isolation are given in Table 2.4, along with an example of these used in a phrase in which the first word now appears utterance-medially.

Whereas the word *ně* is pronounced with a H tone in isolation, when used utterance-medially, the floating H tone appears on a following L tone syllable causing the word *dubǎ* to be pronounced *dúbǎ*.

---

[2]One additional attested tonal pattern not shown here, LH L, is found only in loanwords, e.g. *mǎle* 'compadre', *ŏra* 'hour'.

Table 2.4: Morphemes with floating H tone

Monosyllabic	Disyllabic
ně	*dubă*
[ně:]	[dù:bă:]
L H̄	L L H̄
'and'	'maguey'

Used utterance-medially
ne dúbă
'and maguey'

Finally, it is important to note that the various surface tone types are not all manifested with equal regularity. Pickett's *Vocabulario* (Pickett 1979) reports a frequency of 6% for words that contain a syllable with a high (H) tone, 22% for words that contain a rising (LH) tone, and 17% that contain a floating H tone. Words containing only low (L) tone syllables are the most common, comprising about 55% of the lexical inventory. In the next section, I explore the place of the ZAI tonal system within the broader prosodic system of the language.

2.2 The structural function of prosody in ZAI

This section is concerned with the structural function of prosody in ZAI, that is, with the role of prosody in the segmentation of the speech signal into groups of words. In what follows, I first present a more detailed account of the ZAI phonological system than that provided in §2.1 by offering a summary of the interrelationships between tone, laryngealization, glottalization, and stress. After a short review of the existing literature on the structural function of prosody in other Zapotec languages, I then explore some of the ways that tone, laryngealization, glottalization, and stress interact within the ZAI prosodic system. Finally, I touch briefly on the role of prosody in the marking of information structure, a discussion that will be taken up again in more detail in §5.

2.2.1 Tones, VQMs and stress

Morphemes in ZAI may be either monosyllabic or disyllabic. As was shown above, ZAI has three phonemic tones: high (H), rising (LH), and low (L), as well as two voice quality modifications (VQMs), laryngealization and glottalization, that may participate in lexical contrasts.

In addition, stress, although not lexically contrastive, also plays a key role in ZAI phonology. As a rule, there is only one stressed, double-moraic segment within each phonological word. In disyllabic words, stress falls on the initial syllable. Stressed syllables generally contain long vowels. There are two cases, however, in which the characteristically long, stressed vowel does not occur: 1) if the post-tonic syllable begins with a voiceless obstruent, a nasal, a liquid or a glide which undergoes gemination (geminates are not contrastive in ZAI), as in the di-syllabic words *mǐlǐ* [mǐl:ǐ:] 'mullet' and *chupǎ* [chup:ǎ:] 'two'; or 2) if the morpheme is glottalized, as in the disyllabic word *bé'ñe'* [béʔñeʔ] 'alligator', in which case stress is heard only as heightened intensity and raised pitch register. In short, when stressed, the ZAI syllable nucleus may either be a long vowel (V:), a vowel plus a lengthened consonant (VC:), a laryngealized vowel (VV), or a glottalized vowel (V'). Clitics do not bear stress and maintain a CV structure.

Table 2.5 summarizes the interactions between tones, laryngealization, glottalization, and stress in stressed monosyllabic and disyllabic morphemes (for words uttered in isolation).

If a morpheme is stressed, stress falls on the initial syllable. Duration is the primary phonetic indicator of stress as the stressed syllable must be heavy: either the vocalic nucleus is long or the post-tonic consonant is fortis (a geminate) leaving the vocalic nucleus short. Pre-pause syllables are also long.

However, three additional observations are important to note. First, when we compare morphemes in stressed and unstressed contexts, we see that the shortened syllables in unstressed and utterance-medial positions carry fewer tones. In particular, LH contour tones only arise on long syllables, i.e. on syllables that are either stressed or before a pause. When unstressed, the syllable nucleus is only a single vowel and the contour tones are 'simplified' to a level H tone. This strongly suggests that the mora is the tone-bearing unit (TBU) and that the most appropriate representation is most likely one in which contours are composed of a sequence of level H and L tones linked to the mora. Second, the data also suggest that the L tone is the more unmarked of the two tones. In addition to being the most distributionally unrestricted tone, L is also always the one that is

Table 2.5: Tone, laryngealization and glottalization (in words uttered in isolation) (underline notes the stressed syllable in disyllabic roots).

	plain		glottalized		laryngealized	
H tone	*dxé:* H 'boy'	*lé:xu:* H L 'rabbit'	*ri-ndá'* L H 'gets hot'	*na-yaná'* L L H 'hot/spicy'		
				na-ya'ní' L L H 'clear'		
LH tone	*dxǐ:* LH 'quiet'	*yǔ:zě:* LH LH 'livestock'	*ri-ndǎ'* L LH 'gets bitter'		*nǔu* LH 'there is'	*nadxǐibǐ:* L LH LH 'fearful'
L⌐H⌐ tone	*ně:* L⌐H⌐ 'and'	*du:bǎ:* L L⌐H⌐ 'maguey'			*bǔu* L⌐H⌐ 'charcoal'	*ridxiichǐ:* L L L⌐H⌐ 'be angry'
L tone	*ru:* L 'cough'	*ben:da:* L L 'fish'	*ri-nda'* L L 'stinks'	*na-ya'qui'* L L L 'burnt'	*chii* L 'ten'	*nadxiibi'* L L L 'smooth'

deleted in contour tone 'simplification'.[3]

Furthermore, this raises an important question about the relationship between the realization of contour tone and the structuring function of prosody in ZAI discourse: if contour tones in ZAI only occur on stressed syllables and before a pause, what is the distribution of stress and of pauses at the phrase- or discourse-level? Are they predictable? These questions are addressed in the following sections. First, I briefly review previous studies on Zapotec prosody.

---

[3]Stress and tone have been argued to be closely interrelated in a number of languages (for general discussion, see Yip 2002; Zhang 2002). In particular, pitch movement has been shown to be more common under stress (Zhang 2002; Zoll 2003). This is also true in ZAI as contour tones are shown to commonly surface on stressed syllables. An additional manifestation of this is that stressed L tones have a phonetically falling pitch whereas unstressed syllables with L tone are phonetically level tones.

2.2.2 Previous studies on Zapotec prosody

To my knowledge, the only extensive study that has been done on phrase-level prosody in a Zapotecan language has been the work of Mark Sicoli (2007; 2010). In his PhD dissertation, *A linguistic ethnography of tone and voice in a Zapotec region*, Sicoli devotes two chapters to an analysis of prosody in Lachixío Zapotec (Eastern Zapotec) at both the word level and the phrase level. Although Lachixío Zapotec and ZAI are only distantly related, it is not surprising that many of Sicoli's observations with respect to prosodic structure hold for ZAI as well.

He describes Lachixío Zapotec as a "stress-timed" language where there is only primary (no secondary) stress which is non-iterative, that is, has at most one stress foot. In addition, Sicoli notes that emphasis is marked by a geminate medial consonant or stressed vowel of the primary stress foot and that this can serve focus functions by marking the edge of a phrase.

Based on these observations, Sicoli goes on to analyze the intonational system as composed of four nested levels: the phonological word, the metrical foot, the intermediate phrase, and the intonation phrase. The maximal phonological word is composed of a clitic phrase with the following structure: [[proclitic [stressed root]] enclitic]. The metrical foot, the unit counted for rhythm, is trochaic. The intermediate phrase, a unit between the intonation phrase and the phonological word, is defined by phonetic cues such as phrase-final, non-phonemic lengthening. The intonation phrase is defined prosodically by the structure of boundary tones (phrase-final intonation patterns) and by optional cues, such as pause, breath, and non-phonemic lengthening of phrase-final vowels.

Aside from boundary tones, such as a L boundary tone that marks the ends of speakers' turns and a H boundary tone that indicates non-finality, two factors show that phonological phrasing can have morphosyntactic functions in Zapotec speech: 1) case is unmarked morphologically; and 2) body part nouns may combine with other nouns to form locational expressions (Sicoli 2007: 132).

Sicoli provides an illustrative example of the second one of these factors. In Lachixío Zapotec intermediate phrases help to distinguish between NPs that are grouped together as phonological phrases and those that form separate phonological phrases; this is most clearly seen in the use of body part nouns in "quasi-prepositional" phrases (2007: 133).[4] For example, the two-noun phrase *lattsa níkko* (lit. chest + dog) can be either a possessive construction meaning 'the chest of a dog' or a locational construction meaning 'the side of a dog' (2007: 134). In the possessive structure, the H final intermediate phrase tone is placed at the end of

---

[4]For more work on body part nouns in Zapotec see e.g. MacLaury (1989); Lillehaugen (2006).

the first word (the possessed object), grouping these words as two phonological phrases [[lattsa:][nikko]]. For the locational reading, the second word receives a H final phrase tone that groups these words as a single phonological phrase [lattsa níkko], thus indicating a prepositional use.[5] Compensatory lengthening provides another phonetic cue.

2.2.3 Prosodic properties of intonation units in ZAI

Otomanguean languages have long engaged researchers in the study of the phonetic realization and phonological complexity of stress, tone and vowel phonation (Arellanes 2009; Avelino 2004; Chávez Peón 2010; Mock 1988; *inter alia*). With the objective of understanding in detail the interaction between stress, tone and vowel phonation at the word or root level, the main sources of data for these studies have been words and phrases elicited in isolation. This section complements this growing body of work by presenting a preliminary analysis of the sound patterns in intonation units in ZAI, using naturally-occurring data as evidence.

To recap, ZAI has conserved a CV(CV) structure at the root level. Vowels bear one of three tones - low (the most frequent), high, and rising - and have three phonation types - modal, glottalized and laryngealized. At the root and word level, stress is assigned predictably to the first syllable of the root. The vowel of the stressed syllable is short when the following consonant is fortis, and long when the following consonant is lenis. Various types of extrametrical units can attach to a root, including tense, aspect and mood prefixes as well as pronominal enclitics, yet stress assignment remains dependent on the root structure. In discourse, however, stress and vowel phonation may undergo lenition under certain circumstances. It is this process and the resulting patterns that are the focus here.

In this section, as in the remainder of the study, I use the "intonation unit" (IU) (Chafe 1994) as the basis for transcription and analysis. The reason for this is that IUs have been shown to operate as a fundamental unit of cognitive processing, social interaction, and other domains (Chafe 1994; Du Bois et al. 1993; *inter alia*). To recognize boundaries between IUs, I follow Du Bois et al. (1993: 100) in identifying five major perceptual and acoustic cues: (1) a coherent or unified into-

---

[5]Sicoli also takes this as evidence for the existence of intermediate phrase tones as opposed to intonational pitch accents since they occur at the end of the phrase on an unstressed syllable. Mock (1988: 204), in her analysis of ZAI phonology, in fact uses a similar example as evidence that "words in ZAI need not receive stress since stress ultimately occurs for discourse-related reasons." She does not, however, elaborate on this point.

nation contour; (2) a resetting of the baseline pitch level at the beginning of the unit (pitch reset); (3) a pause between two units; (4) a sequence of accelerated syllables at the beginning of the unit (anacrusis); and (5) a prosodic lengthening of the syllables at the end of the unit.[6] This last cue, IU-final lengthening, is especially relevant for ZAI: the delimitation of IUs in ZAI is aided by the fact that glottalized and laryngealized vowels in IU-final position are immune to the lenition process.

Chafe (1994) distinguishes between three types of IUs: 1) substantive, 2) regulatory and 3) fragmentary. The analysis that follows will focus on the prosodic properties that can be observed in substantive IUs, that is, IUs that convey ideas about events, states, or referents that participate in the communication of propositional content. The data in my corpus shows that, in substantive IUs, stress – whose main phonetic correlate I assume to be duration – resides in the last root of each constituent in a clause and lenites in all other elements towards the left.

Consider the brief sequence of substantive IUs in (3). The first line shows the superficial phonetic representation and the second line shows the morpheme-by-morpheme underlying representation.

(3) 01 racá gidáa   nisa lunĭ
         raca^H gui^{LH}-daa nisa lu=ni^{LH}
         then IMP-empty water face=3SG

         'Then empty water in it,'

     02 guiába   chupa   chóna   xúba luni   lá
         gui^{LH}-yaba chupa^{LH} chonna^{LH} xuba' lu=ni^{LH} la^H
         IMP-fall   two   three   corn face=3SG LA

         'Add a few kernels of corn to it,'

Stress is realized on the first syllable of the last root of each main verb and each argument NP. In the first line, stress falls on the verb root *-daa* 'to empty'. This is observed in the rearticulated vowel, which is fully realized. Stress also falls on the first syllable of *nisa* 'water', which contains a modal vowel that is short, followed by a lengthened fortis consonant. The body-part term *lu* 'face', as head of the locative phrase, also receives stress and the modal vowel is therefore long. In the second line, stress falls again on the first syllable of the verb root, *-yaba* 'fall', and on the first syllable of *xuba'* 'corn'. These two words also contain long modal vowels.

---

[6]It is important to note that the presence of any of these is neither a sufficient nor a necessary condition, as many may occur for reasons other than an IU boundary and some may be difficult to identify under certain conditions.

Other words, such as connectives (e.g. *racá* 'then' in line 1 and modifiers (e.g. *chupa chonna* 'a few' (lit. 'two, three') in line 2 are not stressed. Because stress does not fall on modifiers, the fortis consonants following the modal vowels ([p] in *chupa* and [nn] in *chonna*) are not fully lengthened. This can be seen if we compare them to the fortis consonant in *nisa*, in line 1, which does receive stress and is thereby considerably longer (146ms for /s/ in *nisa* vs. 84ms for /p/ in *chupa* and 75ms for /n/ in *chonna*). Note also that the modal vowel of the unstressed pronominal clitic =*ni* '3SG' is lengthened in IU-final position, 151ms in line 1, but is short otherwise, 59ms in line 2. Similarly, =*ni* carries an underlying rising tone with a floating H and is pronounced with a rising tone in line 1 when lengthened in IU-final position, but is pronounced with a low tone when short in line 2 (and the H tone floats to the following syllable).

What emerges from an analysis of IU sequences such as that in (3), is that stress in ZAI is predictable at the word or root level and is likewise predictable within substantive IUs. The relevant generalization can be stated in terms of syntactic constituency: the last root of each VP or NP constituent receives stress and stress lenites in all other elements to the left.

2.2.4 Prosody in ZAI information structure: some initial remarks

In the previous sections, I briefly described the phonology of ZAI, including its tonal system, with high, rising and low contrastive tones. As was seen, this tonal system interacts in complex ways with vowel phonation and a fortis-lenis distinction in consonants. In addition, I observed that stress operates at the phrase level, concluding that the last root of each VP or NP constituent receives stress and that stress lenites in all other elements to the left.

This basic understanding of the phonological system of ZAI will make it possible in Chapter 5 to investigate the contribution of prosody to information structure in ZAI. There, I will take up the question of whether topic and focus constituents have a constant prosodic realization and whether stresses and pauses are involved in the realization of topic and focus structures. Since one common strategy in languages to communicate the status of a referent as new or focused is via pitch accent, one goal in that chapter will be to determine whether this strategy is available in ZAI as well. We will see, however, that the extent to which phonetic and intonational cues play a role in the expression of information structure in ZAI is minimal and that information structural categories and relations are expressed mainly through the manipulation of constituent order.

In the next section, I move on to a review of verb and clause structure and of constituent order correlations in ZAI. This will complete the brief description of the typological characteristics of the language that will set the foundation for the analysis in the remainder of the study.

2.3 Clause structure and constituent order correlations in ZAI

This section begins with a review of basic verbal morphology. It then addresses the question of constituent order correlations in ZAI to determine whether the language exhibits tendencies that correlate with V-O order rather than with O-V order, as has been claimed for most, if not all, Zapotec languages. I conclude the section, and the chapter, by examining the role that constituent order may play in the expression of information structure and present data that identifies the pre-verbal position as the locus for a variety of discourse functions, including the expression of topic and focus relations.

2.3.1 Verbal morphology

Like most verb-initial languages, ZAI employs verbal prefixes. Verbs obligatorily inflect for tense-aspect-mood (TAM). In addition to TAM, verbs also inflect optionally for causative.[7] Also, if the subject is not a full NP, the verb can be followed by a subject pronominal clitic. The basic order of the morphemes in the ZAI verb can be represented as follows:

ASPECT-(CAUSATIVE)-root-(MODIFIER)=(SUBJECT CLITIC)

Verb roots may belong to one of four verb classes, based on the aspectual prefixes they can combine with. Detailed studies of the morphophonemics of ZAI verb classes are provided in Marlett & Pickett (1987), Enríquez Licón (2008), and Pérez Báez (2015).[8]

---

[7]Overall there is a tendency for suffixes to be associated with OV languages and prefixes with VO languages. However, this is only a unidirectional correlation: if all affixes in the language are suffixes, the language is more likely to be OV. This correlation is not a strong one, and prefixes in OV languages are not at all rare. In other words, we can say that OV languages more commonly have suffixes, but we cannot say that VO languages more commonly have prefixes (Dryer 2007).

[8]For other foundational work on Zapotecan verb classes, see Smith-Stark (2002) and Campbell (2011).

A few additional comments are in order with respect to the TAM prefix.[9] Table 2.6 provides a list of the eight aspectual prefixes found in ZAI as well as a short summary of some of the observations made by previous scholars.

Table 2.6: ZAI Tense-Aspect-Mood system

Prefix	TAM	Description/Example
ri-, ru-	Habitual	Used for habitual or repeated actions in past or present, but never future
bi-, gu-	Completive	For finished actions, typically in past but not necessarily (e.g. future perfect)
ca-, cu-	Progressive	For continuing actions in past, present or future but may be temporal when used for future
za-, zu-	Future	For future actions not yet begun, certain
ni-, nu-, ñ-	Irrealis	For something that is contrary to fact; for something that did not happen
gui-, gu-	Potential	Future action in relation to the time indicated by the main verb or in relation to utterance time used for subordinate clauses also, 'to want' or 'to like to' (in the future) in some imperative constructions
hua-	Perfect	For past actions that have occurred more than once, also used in the negative to show a time during which something has not happened
na-	Stative	Forms a stative verb, more limited distribution occurs with about half of the roots

For the purposes of this study, the TAM prefix will be referred to as an aspectual prefix, but no claim is being made as to the specific syntactic-semantic function of these prefixes and a complete analysis of the ZAI TAM system is outside the scope of this project.

---

[9]Pickett et al. (1998) describes the ZAI TAM system as essentially an aspectual system with only one tense prefix (future). Mock (1990) describes the system as just aspect and mood, while Suárez (1983) describes the system as one that combines tense, aspect and mood. A complete study of the ZAI TAM system would be extremely valuable (see Pérez Báez (2015); also Sicoli (2015) for the TAM system of Lachixío Zapotec .

Finally, it should also be noted that there is no morphological case marking on nouns and there is no agreement between the verb and any of its arguments. Some features of ZAI that are canonical of most verb-initial languages are: adjectives generally follow nouns, possessive constructions are possessor final, and the use of prepositions rather than postpositions. I address constituent order correlations further in the next section, where I analyze the position of the verb with respect to the direct object.

2.3.2 Constituent order correlations

Previous research on ZAI has claimed that the most common arrangement of constituents is verb followed by the subject then any objects (Pickett 1960; Pickett et al. 1998).[10] Verb-initial languages are much less common than verb-final languages (Payne 1995). However, it is also generally understood that "no languages are rigidly verb-initial in the same sense that some languages are rigidly verb-final." (E. Keenan, quoted in Payne (1995: 455)). These two facts make the study of constituent order and of verb-initial languages challenging as there are well-known problems with establishing the relevant criteria to determine the basic constituent order in a language. Salient among these are two particular difficulties: 1) the order of subject and verb and the order of object and verb are often easier to identify while the order of subject and object is often more difficult to identify; and 2) pronouns may exhibit constituent order properties that differ considerably from lexical noun phrases.

In determining these patterns for a language, should the relevant criterion be one of frequency, of distribution, or of pragmatics? In constituent order typology, frequency has been the primary criterion used (Dryer 2007). It can be argued that differences in frequency often provide a more reliable test than other tests (where the difference is large enough). However, differences in frequency might be an artifact of a particular set of texts, due to genre specific or speaker idiosyncracies, for example, and one might therefore find very different frequencies in a different set of texts. Also, frequency counts of some languages may not reveal one order as noticeably more frequent than the other. Additionally, it can also be argued that because it is not part of the grammar of the language, frequency should not be used widely as a criterion (Dryer 2007).

---

[10]The same is true for most if not all Zapotec languages (see e.g. Lee 2000 for San Lucas Quiavini Zapotec (Central); Beam de Azcona (2004) for Coatlán-Loxicha Zapotec (Southern); Sonnenschein (2005) for San Bartolomé Zoogocho Zapotec (Northern); Sicoli (2007) for Lachixío Zapotec (Eastern)).

A criterion of distribution refers to whether the fact that one order, found to be in some way less restricted in its distribution, can be used as an argument that it is more basic than another, more restricted order. In a similar fashion, one order in a language may be considered pragmatically neutral and another to have some added pragmatic effect. However, it may not be obvious that one order adds any additional elements and, instead, the two orders may simply have a difference in meaning (e.g. OV order may be associated with indefinite objects and VO order with definite ones).

In this section, I analyze the correlates of various grammatical elements with the relative order of verb and object in order to determine a tendency in ZAI toward either verb-object (VO) order or object-verb (OV) order. As will be seen, all but two of the elements correlate with a VO order, as would be expected. The section that follows will discuss the subject position and will show that the exceptions to the V(S)O order are the ones that are pragmatically marked.

The universal tendencies associated with OV versus VO order are found in languages in which there is considerable flexibility of constituent order, even among languages in which one order outnumbers the other by a frequency of only 2 to 1 (Dryer 2007). These elements are listed in Table 2.7.

Examples for each are provided in the following discussion.

2.3.2.1 Use of prepositions

ZAI uses prepositional phrases, as in the following two examples:

(4) má   bietebe   dé lu   yaga quě
     ma'^{H} bi-yete=be^{LH} de lu   yaga que^{LH}
     already COMPL-descend=3.HUM PP face tree DIST
     'He already came down from on the tree.'

(5) cuchabe   cáni   ndáani ti   lari
     c.u-cha=be^{LH} ca=ni^{LH} ndaani ti   lari
     PROG.CAUS-fill=3.HUM PL=3.INAN PP   one cloth
     'He (was) putting them in a shirt.'

Prepositions in ZAI, if they are not borrowed from Spanish, are body part terms.[11] In (4), the body part term *lu* 'face' is used as part of the prepositional phrase *de lu yaga que* 'from on the tree' (lit. 'from face tree that'). In this case,

---

[11] For more on the use of body-part terms in Zapotec languages, see e.g. MacLaury (1989) and Pérez Báez (2011).

Table 2.7: Elements whose order correlates strongly with that of verb and object (Dryer 2007)

OV	VO
postpositions	prepositions
adpositional phrase – verb	verb – adpositional phrase
genitive – noun	noun – genitive
manner adverb – verb	verb – manner adverb
standard – marker	marker – standard
standard – adjective	adjective – standard
final adverbial subordinator	initial adverbial subordinator
main verb – auxiliary verb	auxiliary verb – main verb
predicate – copula	copula – predicate
final question particle	initial question particle
final complementizer	initial complementizer
noun – article	article – noun
noun – plural marker	plural marker – noun
subordinate clause – main clause	main clause – subordinate clause
relative clause – noun	noun – relative clause

the prepositional phrase is headed by the preposition *de* borrowed from Spanish. In (5), the body part term *ndaani* 'stomach' functions as the prepositional head of the phrase *ndaani ti lari* 'in a shirt' (lit. 'stomach one shirt').

2.3.2.2 Adpositional phrase placed after the verb

The examples in (4) and (5) demonstrate that the position of adpositional phrases is after the verb, as expected for a language whose basic order is VO.

2.3.2.3 Genitive follows the possessed noun

As would be expected in a language with VO order, lexical genitives follow possessed nouns in ZAI, as in (6):

(6) cayaadxa   ti dxumi   pĕra   badunguiiu
     ca-yaadxa'   ti dxumi^{LH} pe^{LH}ra badunguiiu
     PROG-be.missing one basket pear   man

'One of the man's baskets of pears was missing.'

In the complex subject NP, *ti dxumi pera badunguiiu*, the lexical genitive *badunguiiu* 'man' appears after the possessed noun *ti dxumi pera* 'a basket of pears.'
  In addition, possessive pronoun clitics also follow possessed nouns, as in (7):

(7) bidxí'babe   lú   xpiciclétabĕ
     bi-dxi'^{H}ba=be^{LH} lu   x-bicicle^{H}ta=be^{LH}
     COMPL-climb.up=3.HUM face POSS=bicycle=3.HUM

'He got on his bicycle.'

Here, the third-person subject clitic *=be* appears as an enclitic on the possessed noun *bicicleta* 'bicycle', to which the possessive prefix *x-* attaches.

2.3.2.4 Manner adverbs follow the verb

Manner adverbs may follow the verb, as in (8), where the adverb *nachaahui'* appears after the verb:

(8) biluxebe   náchaahui'
     bi-luxe=be^{LH} na-chaahui'
     COMPL-finish=3.HUM STAT-well

'S/he finished well.'

They may also attach directly to the end of the verb root, as modifiers, as in (9):

(9) gátachaahui   ira   guétabaadxi că
     g^{LH}-a'ta-chaahui' guira^{LH} guetabaadxi ca^{LH}
     IMP-lay-well   all   tamal   DEM

'Lay down all the tamales carefully.'

  In example (9), the verb root *a'ta* 'lay down' contains a glottalized vowel that is pronounced when stressed. In this case, the adverb *chaahui'* appears immediately after the verb root and stress falls not on the verb root but on the adverb, as it is the rightmost element of the verbal constituent. Stress lenites in all elements to the left, as we saw in §2.2.3.

There are, however, cases in which an adverb may appear before the verb, as in (10):

(10) nachaahui   bíluxebě
      na-chaahui' bi-luxe=be^{LH}
      STAT-well   COMPL-finish=3.HUM
      'S/he finished WELL.'

Cases such as this occur when information carried by the verb is presupposed and the manner adverb is asserted, or focused (cf. 8). These cases are pragmatically-marked in the sense of Payne (1995), as I will explore in §2.3.5.

Variation in the relative position of main clause and adverbial clause is common in ZAI, as in many languages. Conditional clauses, for example, exhibit a universal tendency to precede the main clause (Haiman 1978). In this study, I consider this variation to be related to discourse pragmatics and to the communication of topical information. This will be explored in more detail in Chapter 6, where the issue of subordinate adverbial clauses will be tied closely to the analysis of the LA particle, which is the topic of §6.2.

2.3.2.5 Order in comparative constructions is adjective-marker-standard

The comparative construction currently used in ZAI, with the order adjective-marker-standard, is a construction borrowed from the Spanish *más que*. An example is shown in (11):

(11) jmá nahuinni   jñaabe   qué bixhozebě
      jma^H na-huinni jñaa=be^{LH} que bixhoze=be^{LH}
      more STAT-small mother=3.HUM   than father=3.HUM
      'His/her mother is younger than his/her father.'

The order here is adjective-marker-standard. The native ZAI comparative construction has not yet been documented. However, in San Lucas Quiaviní Zapotec, a central Zapotec language, the native comparative construction appears to also have an adjective-marker-standard order (Galant 2006), as in (12):

(12) Zyuùa'-ru' Lia Oli'eb loh Rrodriiegw.
      tall-ER   Ms. Olivia than Rodrigo
      'Olivia is taller than Rodrigo.'

It is likely that the native ZAI comparative construction would be similar.

2.3.2.6 Initial adverbial subordinator

ZAI has a long list of adverbial subordinators, all of which have been borrowed from Spanish: *ora, lugar de, ante, dede, cada, para, cumu, modo, sinuque, sin*. All adverbial subordinators occur at the beginning of the subordinate clause. Some examples are:

(13) ŏrá cá lá, má áca licuărnĭ
o^{LH}ra ca^{LH} la^{H} ma'^{H} g^{LH}-aca licua^{LH}r=ni^{LH}
when DEM LA already IMP-become blend=3SG.INAN

'At that time, blend it.'

(14) ănte de las ŏcho chuudŭ
a^{LH}nte de las o^{LH}cho ch-uu=du^{LH}
before of the eight POT-go=1PL.EXCL

'Before eight we go.'

(15) pŭrti má las ŏcho de la mañăna chuuzulu
pu^{LH}rti ma'^{H} las o^{LH}cho de la maña^{LH}na chuu-zulu=∅
because already the eight of the morning POT.go-begin=3SG.INAN

'Because already at eight in the morning it was going to begin.'

As with the comparative construction, it is likewise unclear what the native clause-combining strategy is; perhaps one of juxtaposition, but this is conjecture and requires further study.

2.3.2.7 Auxiliary verb precedes main verb

A minority of verbs can occur as auxiliary verbs. When they do, they appear before the main verb. One example is *-anda* 'be able to' in (16), followed by the main verb:

(16) ¿zanda ígánitú lá?
z-anda^{LH} gui^{LH}-gani^{LH}=tu^{LH} la^{H}
FUT-be.able POT-be.silent=2PL Q

'Can you (all) be quiet?

2.3.2.8 Copula precedes the predicate

There is no copular construction in ZAI. However, nonverbal predicates occur at
the beginning of the clause, as in the following example:

(17) mecănico   laabĕ
      meca^{LH}nico laa=be^{LH}
      mechanic   BASE=3.HUM

      'He is a mechanic.'

2.3.2.9 Question particles

Interrogative expressions in content questions in verb-initial languages most
commonly occur at the beginning of sentences. This is true in ZAI as well. In
the examples below, the question words *panda* 'how many' in (18) and *pabia'*
'how much' in (19) occur sentence-initially:

(18) ¿panda   kílŏmetru   bixooñelu   raquĕ?
      panda^{LH} kilo^{LH}metru bi-xooñe'=lu'   raque^{LH}
      how.many kilometer   COMPL-run=2SG then

      'How many kilometers did you run?'

(19) ¿pabiá   ruxooñelu   ira   dxí ya?
      pabia'^{H} ru-xooñe-lu' guira^{LH} dxi ya
      how.much HAB-run=2SG all   day Q

      'How much do you run every day?'

Yes/no question particles in verb-initial languages most often also occur at the
beginning of the sentence. In ZAI, however, such a particle is not obligatory and,
in fact, is rarely used. The final particle LA is required in yes/no questions:

(20) ¿(ñée) biiyalu   laabe   lá?
      ñee^{H} bi-uuya=lu'   laa=be^{LH} la^{H}
      Q   COMPL-see=2SG BASE=3.HUM LA

      'Did you see him/her?'

The question *¿ñée biiyalu laabe?*, without the LA particle, would be ungrammati-
cal. [12]

---

[12] One of the hypotheses examined in more detail in Chapter 6 is that the yes/no question particle
LA is related to the LA particle involved in the marking of topical information.

2.3.2.10 Initial complementizer

There is no overt complementizer in ZAI. An example is shown in (21):

(21) binadiaagá   binda   ti   gaayu
      bi-nadiaaga=a'[H] bi-nda   ti   gaayu
      COMPL-hear=1SG COMPL-sing one rooster
      'I heard a rooster sing.'

2.3.2.11 Article appears before the noun

It is common for the article to precede the noun in VO languages.[13] There are no articles in ZAI. However, quantifiers such as *ti* 'one' (22) and *ca* PL (23) may precede the noun:

(22) ti   badunguiiu
      ti   badunguiiu
      one man
      'one/a man'

(23) ca badunguiiu
      ca badunguiiu
      PL man
      'men'

Both of these NPs are indefinite. To mark definiteness, ZAI employs demonstratives, which must appear after the noun:

(24) ti   badunguiiu quě
      ti   badunguiiu que[LH]
      one man   DIST
      'that man'

(25) ca badunguiiu quě
      ca badunguiiu que[LH]
      PL man   DIST
      'those men'

---

[13] An additional, though weaker, correlation is that articles appear to be somewhat more common in VO languages than they are in OV languages.

Unlike articles, the position of demonstratives does not exhibit a cross-linguistic correlation with respect to the order of object and verb. The use of demonstratives in discourse will be explored in more detail in Chapter 3.

2.3.2.12 Plural marker - noun

The plural marker *ca* always precedes the noun in ZAI, as was shown in (23).

2.3.2.13 Main clause - subordinate clause

Many languages, including ZAI, exhibit considerable freedom in the position of subordinate clauses. In some cases, adverbial subordinate clauses in ZAI can precede the main clause, as was seen in (13)-(15). However, complement clauses follow the main clause, as shown here (cf. (26)-(27)):

(26) racaladxi   Juán guéedá   Míguél íxí'
      ri=aca-ladxi   Juan^H gu^{LH}=eeda^{LH} Miguel^H guixi'^{H}
      HAB=occur-gut Juan POT=come   Miguel tomorrow

      'Juan wants Miguel to come tomorrow.'

(27) na Juán biiya   Miguél   ca xcuídí quě
      na Juan^H bi=uuya Miguel^H ca xcui^{H}di que^{LH}
      say Juan   Miguel COMPL=see PL child   DIST

      'Juan said Miguel saw the children.'

2.3.2.14 Noun - relative clause

Almost all VO languages place the relative clause after the noun, as illustrated in (28). Here, the relative clause *ni riree ndaani yuze* 'that comes out of the stomach of the cow' follows the NP *cuaju ca* 'the rennet':

(28) cuǎju   ca   ní riree   ndaani yǔzě
      cua^{LH}ju ca^{LH} ni ri-ree   ndaani   yu^{LH}ze^{LH}
      rennet   DEM REL HAB-leave stomach cow

      'The rennet that comes out of the stomach of the cow.'

2.3.3 Summary of constituent order correlations

The above discussion has shown that the great majority of the constituent order correlations in Table 2.7 conforms to a pattern of verb-object in ZAI. A summary of these correlations in ZAI and how they are manifested is presented in Table 2.8.

Table 2.8: Correlations between verb and object order in ZAI

VO order correlations	ZAI
prepositions	✓
verb - adpositional phrase	✓
noun - genitive	✓
verb - manner adverb	Variable, obeys discourse motivations
marker - standard	✓ (*native construction unknown)
adjective - standard	✓ (*native construction unknown)
initial adverbial subordinator	Variable, obeys discourse motivations
auxiliary verb - main verb	✓
copula - predicate	No copula
initial question particle	Yes/no particle appears clause-finally
initial complementizer	✓
article - noun	No articles
plural marker - noun	✓
main clause - subordinate clause	Variable, obeys discourse motivations
noun - relative clause	✓

While the majority of the constituent order correlations discussed conform to cross-linguistic tendencies for VO languages, it is worth noting the exceptions here. First, there are no copula or articles in ZAI. Second, the principal rigid exception is the yes/no question particle LA, which appears utterance-finally rather than, as would be expected for an VO language, utterance-initially. This particle will be analyzed in more detail in §6.2. Finally, several constituent order correlations show variation. We saw that in the cases of the manner adverb - verb or main clause - subordinate clause, the order obeys specific discourse motivations.

These motivations will be explored more fully in Chapters 5 and 6. The next section follows up this discussion of constituent order by focusing more specifically on the pre-verbal position, which we know to be a prominent position cross-linguistically and, in particular, in verb-initial languages.

2.3.4 The pre-verbal position and rigidity in verb-initial syntax

In her analysis of the pragmatic properties of verb-initial languages, Payne (1995) surveys the discourse functions that constituents may have in pre-verbal position. She groups these functions under the label "pragmatically marked", that is, "information which is to some degree counter to what the speaker assumes are the hearer's current expectations or presuppositions" (Payne 1995: 110). Payne argues that there exists a continuum for pragmatically marked (PM) information which includes, on one end, information that is contrary to hearer's assumptions and, on the other, information in accord with or only incrementally different from the hearer's expectations. Based on this observation, Payne proposes a hierarchy of pragmatic markedness, represented in Table 2.9:

Table 2.9: A hierarchy of pragmatic markedness (Payne 1995: 479)

more marked	>	less marked
NP in descriptive or background clause	> NP establishing a foundation >	Pragmatically marked NPs

According to this hierarchy, if a verb-initial language places phrases before the verb to accomplish any function to the left on the following hierarchy, all phrases that accomplish functions to the right on the hierarchy will also occur before the verb. That is, among PM phrases, if a verb-initial language places a somewhat more marked phrase type before the verb, then it will also place less marked types before the verb. Languages that fall to the left on this hierarchy are clearly less rigidly verb-initial than are languages to the right.

As will become clear from the following discussion, however, ZAI is not a rigidly verb-initial language. Indeed, all of the elements in the hierarchy – from descriptive and background clauses to pragmatically-marked NPs – can appear in pre-verbal position. I discuss the pre-verbal position in more detail in the next section as this is an important fact, and one that I will return to throughout the analysis in the remainder of this study. It will become especially relevant in

Chapter 5 and Chapter 6, when I discuss the question of the relative "rigidity" of ZAI syntax and its relation to the types of topic and focus constructions available to ZAI speakers.

2.3.5 The pre-verbal position in ZAI

In rigid verb-initial languages, predicates also come first in clauses that are not temporally sequenced, but which serve to introduce and describe referents, state background conditions, or describe events that are out of sequence with the main event line (Payne 1995: 454). An almost universal strategy in verb-initial languages, however, is that if part of a sentence is questioned or is the answer to a question, it will come first. They are, in the words of Payne (1995), "pragmatically marked," in the sense that initial position is associated with novel attention re-direction of some kind. The remaining constituents come at the end.

The pre-verbal position has been identified as a privileged position from the perspective of information structure in other Zapotec languages as well. For example, Broadwell (2002) for San Dionicio Ocotepec Zapotec (Central Zapotec) and Lee (2000) for San Lucas Quiavini Zapotec (Central Zapotec) also identify the pre-verbal position as a topic or focus position. Similarly, Black (2000: 103), in her study of Quiegolani Zapotec (Central Zapotec) syntax, states, "Discourse analyses done on other Zapotecan languages show that the fronted nominal may be either old or new information."

In addition to much of the data already explored above involving constituents in pre-verbal position (cf. adverbial clauses (13)-(15)); also, adjectives, as in (10)), the patterns described below provide further evidence that the pre-verbal position in ZAI is indeed the locus for a variety of discourse functions, such as: question words, negation, focus of contrast (e.g. subject or objects NPs, adjectives), and initiation of new subsections of a text through the (re)introduction of participants.

2.3.5.1 Pre-verbal position: wh-words

As seen above in (18) and (19), the pre-verbal position is reserved for wh-words. Two additional examples are provided here in (29) and (30):

(29) ¿xi bí'nibě?
      xi^{LH} b-i'ni-be^{LH}
      what COMPL-do-3SG
      'What did s/he do?'

(30) ¿tu bí'ni   nǐ?
      tu^{LH} b-i'ni   ni^{LH}
      who COMPL-do 3.INAN
      'Who did it?'

2.3.5.2 Pre-verbal position: negation

Negation in ZAI always precedes the verb, as in (31):

(31) qué reedabé   guírá   dxí
      que^{H} r-eeda^{LH}-be^{LH} guira'^{LH} dxi
      NEG HAB-come-3SG all   day
      'S/He doesn't come every day.'   (Pickett et al. 1998: 78)

2.3.5.3 Pre-verbal position: focus of contrast

Pickett et al. (1998) note that a core argument can be "emphasized" by placing it before the verb. In such constructions, if the argument is a full noun phrase, no co-referring subject clitic pronoun is found on the verb, as shown in (32):

(32) Pědro biiya   ti   badudxaapa
      Pe^{LH}dro bi-uuya   ti   badu-dxaapa
      Pedro COMPL-see INDEF child-woman
      'PEDRO saw a girl.'   (Pickett et al. 1998: 98)

If the argument is a pronominal subject, however, a co-referring dependent pronoun does appear cliticized to the verb, as shown here in (33):

(33) laabe   bí'yabe   tí   badudxaapa
      laa-be^{LH} b-i'ya-be^{LH} ti   badu-dxaapa
      BASE-3SG COMPL-see-3SG INDEF child-woman
      'S/HE saw a girl.'   (Pickett et al. 1998: 98)

Additionally, a construction which places the object in pre-verbal position is also possible in ZAI. For example, in answer to the question 'What did s/he do?' (29), one can respond:

(34) dxiiña bi'nibě
      dxiiña' bi-ini=be^{LH}
      work   COMPL-do=3SG
      'S/He did WORK.'

It is possible, also, to use a similar construction involving the discourse particle, NGA.

(35) dxiiña ngá bi'nibĕ
      dxiiña' ngá bi-ini=be^LH
      work NGA COMPL-do=3SG
      'S/He did WORK.'

In this case, the relevant interpretation is that of an exhaustive listing. A more detailed discussion of this particle will be taken up in §5.1.4.

Although it is not clear what Pickett, et al. refer to by "emphasized", it is clear that the use of an NP in pre-verbal position in each of these cases communicates discourse-pragmatic information. In Chapters 5 and 6, I analyze these constructions as "identificational" or "argument focus" constructions, where only a single NP is focused and the rest of the proposition is within the presupposition (Lambrecht 1994: 228–233). As will be shown, in these cases, the NP in pre-verbal position is not necessarily "new" information, as it is not the focused noun itself which contributes the new information to the discourse, but the relationship between (the referent of) this noun and the entire proposition.

2.3.5.4 Pre-verbal position: left-dislocated phrases

Finally, as will be discussed in more depth in Chapters 3 and 6, some nouns (including independent pronouns) appear in the pre-verbal position and are separated by the particle LA as well as by a pause in the intonation. These are left-dislocated phrases, i.e. phrases that occur under a separate intonation contour, and which may or may not be morphosyntactically related to the verbal case frame. If related, a resumptive reference may occur. These left-dislocated phrases often delimit a time, location, or some other conceptual frame of reference for what follows. By contrast, a non-dislocated pre-verbal phrase may or may not be related to the verbal case frame, but, if it is, a resumptive reference will likely not occur.

2.4 Summary and research questions

In summary, this chapter has described the main phonological and syntactic characteristics at the core of ZAI grammar. It was shown that ZAI is a tonal language, with high, rising and low contrastive tones and that these interact in complex ways with vowel phonation and a fortis-lenis distinction in consonants. It was also shown that stress and tone play a significant role in prosody beyond the word-level. Verb morphology is primarily agglutinative, in that there is no morphological case marking on nouns and there is no agreement between the verb and any of its arguments. I then reviewed the main patterns in constituent order relations in ZAI and showed that the most common arrangement of constituents in ZAI is considered to be verb followed by subject, then object. Finally, many features of ZAI are characteristic of verb-initial languages: adverbial subordinators are clause-initial; presence of prepositions rather than postpositions; adjectives generally follow nouns; possessive constructions are possessor final, etc. However, verb-initial syntax is often violated as the pre-verbal position can be the locus for important discourse functions.

With this background in mind, I devote the chapters that follow to an examination of the interplay between verb-initial order, tone and prosody in ZAI. As has been pointed out, little has been said about the possible phonological, morphological and/or syntactic correlations with the expression of information structure in this language. From the preceding discussion, however, several questions arise that will guide the analysis with respect to four areas: 1) the relation between nominal forms and cognitive status; 2) constituent order; 3) discourse particles; and 4) prosody. I list these questions here:

Nominal forms and cognitive status

- How do the different morphological forms of nominals express different cognitive statuses? How does each cognitive status correlate formally with type of nominal expression?

- To what extent do phonetic and intonational cues play a role in the expression of cognitive status?

Constituent order

- Verb-initial syntax in ZAI is frequently violated in constructions in which topicalized and focalized elements may often appear before the verb. Since constituent order is known to have important discourse functions in many languages and since a small percentage of the world's languages are verb-initial, how does verb-initial syntax in ZAI condition the ways that speakers mark topic and focus?

- Are constituent order changes a possible strategy for expressing all types of topic and focus constructions or only a subset? How pragmatically and syntactically "rigid" is the language?

Discourse particles

- There are two discourse particles, LA and NGA, that are involved in expressing information structure in ZAI. Can the LA form be considered a contrastive topic marker? Is the NGA form involved in the realization of focused material?

- In which cases is the use of these particles infelicitous?

Prosody

- If the realization of contour tones is tied to the realization of stress and of pauses, what is the distribution of stress and of pauses at the phrase- or discourse-level? Are they predictable?

- Are stress and pauses involved in the realization of topic and focus structures? Do topic and focus structures have a constant prosodic realization? In other words, is prosody involved in the realization of topic or focus?

In the next chapter, I take the grammatical information presented here as a basis to address the first group of questions listed above with respect to ZAI nominal and pronominal forms, as well as their potential functions in discourse. In particular, I explore the ways in which different forms may signal different types of cognitive status, terms which will be illustrated below.

3 Preferred Argument Structure and the pragmatic status of nominal forms in ZAI

In the study of information structure, it is necessary to make a distinction between: a) the pragmatic states of the referents of individual sentence constituents in the minds of the speech participants, and b) the pragmatic relations established between these referents and propositions. The focus of this chapter is on the first of these. I will turn to the issue of topic and focus relations in Chapters 5 and 6.

3.1 Preferred Argument Structure in ZAI

This section is concerned with the relationship between the realization of nominal forms and the syntactic role in which they appear. I will frame the analysis using Du Bois's theory of Preferred Argument Structure (Du Bois 1987; Du Bois et al. 2003; Du Bois 2003a,b), with two main goals in mind: 1) to observe the types, frequencies, and syntactic distributions of the nominal forms used by ZAI speakers to satisfy their discursive goals, and 2) to evaluate the capacity of Preferred Argument Structure to account for the patterns observed.

3.1.1 Data and Methodology

The data for this section are made up of narratives elicited from seven ZAI-Spanish bilingual adults between the ages of 25 and 45. To ensure comparability across this and Du Bois and others' work, I asked the consultants to view the Pear film, a short 7-minute film designed for cross-linguistic comparison (Chafe 1980), and then to afterward retell the plot of the story.[1]

---

[1]The four main characters in the Pear film are (the abbreviations follow Chafe 1980): Bike boy, Bike girl, Pear man, and the Three boys. The outline of the Pear Story is reproduced here from Chafe (1980: xiii-xiv) for convenience:

The film begins with a man picking pears on a ladder in a tree. He descends the ladder, kneels, and dumps the pears from the pocket of an apron he is wearing into one of three baskets below

I administered the seven interviews and recorded the narratives in Juchitán. At the time of the interviews I had enough knowledge of the language to carry on basic conversations. The speakers I interviewed were all citizens of Juchitán who I saw and spoke to in Isthmus Zapotec on a daily basis and who made regular attempts to help me listen to and understand normal everyday speech. Therefore, although the situation was somewhat unnatural given my lack of native fluency in the language, I do not think this necessarily compromised the naturalness of the recorded narratives. I later transcribed the narratives myself and corroborated my transcriptions with a native ZAI speaker (not one of the seven participants).

As mentioned in Chapter 2, I use the "intonation unit" (Chafe 1994) as the basis for the transcription as well as for the analysis below. I understand intonation

---

the tree. He removes a bandana from around his neck and wipes off one of the pears. Then he returns to the ladder and climbs back into the tree. Toward the end of this sequence we hear the sound of a goat, and when the picker is back in the tree a man approaches with a goat on a leash. As they pass by the baskets of pears, the goat strains toward them, but is pulled past by the man and the two of them disappear in the distance.

We see another close-up of the picker at this work, and then we see a boy approaching on a bicycle. He coasts in toward the baskets, stops, gets off his bike, looks up at the picker, puts down his bike, walks toward the baskets, again looking at the picker, picks up a pear, puts it back down, looks once more at the picker, and lifts up a basket full of pears. He puts the basket down near his bike, lifts up the bike and straddles it, picks up the basket and places it on the rack in front of his handle bars, and rides off. We again see the man continuing to pick pears.

The boy is now riding down the road, and we see a pear fall from the basket on his bike. Then we see a girl on a bicycle approaching from the other direction. As they pass, the boy turns to look at the girl, his hat flies off, and the front wheel of his bike hits a rock. The bike falls over, the basket falls off, and the pears spill out onto the ground. The boy extricates himself from under the bike, and brushes off his leg.

In the meantime we hear what turns out to be the sound of a paddleball, and then we see three boys standing there, looking at the bike boy on the ground. The three pick up the scattered pears and put them back in the basket. The bike boy sets his bike upright, and two of the other boys lift the basket of pears back onto it. The bike boy begins walking his bike in the direction he was going, while the three other boys begin walking off in the other direction. As they walk by the bike boy's hat on the road, the boy with the paddleball sees it. picks it up, turns around, and we hear a loud whistle as he signals to the bike boy. The bike boy stops, takes three pears out of the basket, and holds them out as the other boy approaches with the hat. They exchange the pears and the hat, and bike boy keeps going while the boy with the paddleball runs back to his two companions, to each of whom he hands a pear. They continue on, eating their pears.

The scene now changes back to the tree, where we see the picker again descending the ladder. He looks at the two baskets, where earlier there were three, points at them, backs up against the ladder, shakes his head, and tips up his hat. The Three boys are now seen approaching, eating their pears. The picker watches them pass by, and they walk off into the distance.

unit to mean the stretch of speech occurring between two specific prosodic cues: an initial pause and a final lengthening. The reason for this is that intonation units have been shown to operate as fundamental units of cognitive processing, social interaction, and other domains, or in Chafe's words, as as representing a single "focus of consciousness" (see also Du Bois et al. 1993). Since intonation units tend to correspond very closely with simple clause structure, we will see in the vast majority of the examples below that the intonation unit tends to overlap with a core clause (i.e. a predicate plus its nominal arguments) in such a way that the arguments of a clause core fit within the single intonation contour delimited by the intonation unit.[2]

This study is based on a total of 346 clauses. The Pear Story was chosen as the method of elicitation because of its conduciveness to cross-linguistic comparison. With the exclusion of first and second person arguments, the analysis concentrates on the variety and distribution of third person forms and involves a quantitative study of the nominal forms, as this allows verification of the recurrent role and quantity tendencies predicted by Preferred Argument Structure and observed in the ZAI narratives. Given that there are no other existing linguistic studies of ZAI discourse, and despite a significant amount of poetry and literature published in the language, the claims here are still preliminary and leave open the question of possible sociolinguistic variation in terms of variables such as genre or dialect.

3.1.2 Evidence for PAS in ZAI

In his theory of Preferred Argument Structure (PAS), Du Bois (1987; 2003a,b) makes specific correlations between discourse patterns and the form of the "core" arguments of the verb. Based on data from narratives in Sakapultek Maya, an ergative language spoken in Guatemala, Du Bois (1987) proposed the set of four closely related grammatical and pragmatic constraints at work in the distribution of arguments in spoken discourse shown in Table 3.1.

Along the pragmatic dimension, the One New Argument Constraint reflects the tendency for no more than one core argument in a clause to contain new information. Another constraint, the Given A Constraint, states that this new information (typically expressed by full lexical noun phrases) freely appears in the intransitive subject position (the S role) or the transitive object position (the

---

[2]There is, however, an important exception to this tendency in the ZAI data presented here. This is the case of "marked topics" or topicalized NPs set off in a separate preceding intonation unit without a verb, which are analyzed in §3.1.7.2.

Table 3.1: Preferred argument structure constraints (Du Bois 2003a: 34)

	Grammar	Pragmatics
Quantity	Avoid more than one lexical core argument "One Lexical Argument Constraint"	Avoid more than one new core argument "One New Argument Constraint"
Role	Avoid lexical A "Nonlexical A Constraint"	Avoid new A "Given A Constraint"

O role), but not in the transitive subject position (the A role).[3] Parallel to this, along the grammatical dimension, the One Lexical Argument Constraint refers to the scarcity of clauses in which more than one core argument is expressed with a full noun phrase, the additional core arguments being expressed with pronouns or zero forms. Finally, the Non-lexical A Constraint reflects the tendency for speakers to freely realize full lexical noun phrases in the intransitive subject position (the S role) or the transitive object position (the O role), but strongly avoid placing them in the transitive subject position (the A role).

Thus, the constraints on role refer to the avoidance of lexical/new transitive subjects and the constraints on quantity refer to the avoidance of more than one lexical/new argument in the same clause. The existence of these constraints has been supported by much empirical cross-linguistic research and this has been accepted by many as evidence that PAS is a universal feature of discourse.

The strong tendency for new and lexical arguments to appear in S and O roles and to avoid the A role, though not a categorical rule, has been shown to occur widely in the spontaneous discourse of many typologically diverse languages (e.g. Hebrew, Sakapultek, Papago, English, Spanish, French, Brazilian Portuguese, Japanese, Achenese, Nepali, Finnish and Mapudungun) and in many genres and contexts (e.g. spoken, written, child interaction) (see Du Bois et al. 2003 and contents therein). That said, there are a number of studies that question the validity of PAS and its universality (see e.g. Haig & Schnell 2016 and Brickell & Schnell 2017 for recent, well-structured, and insightful critiques.)

As will be seen in the following discussion, the tendencies predicted by PAS do occur widely in third-person narratives in ZAI. Table 3.2 summarizes the distribution across the core clause of full lexical noun phrases (LNP).

---

[3]The term "core argument" is used in the sense of Dixon (1979), where A refers to the transitive subject, O to the transitive object, and S to the intransitive subject.

Table 3.2: Lexical arguments in core grammatical roles

	A role	S role	O role	Total
LNP	9% (19/201)	26%(52/201)	65% (130/201)	100% (201/201)

Out of 201 total LNPs in the corpus, only 19 occur in the A role. The pattern of distribution of LNPs obeys the Non-lexical A constraint, as predicted by PAS. The majority of LNPs occur in the O role (65%), followed by the S role (26%) and finally the A role (9%). The rate of lexical mentions in the S role thus falls in between the rate of lexical mentions in the O and A roles. Du Bois (2003b: 37) reports similar patterns found in several other unrelated languages, as seen in Table 3.3:[4]

Table 3.3: A cross-linguistic comparison of lexical arguments in core grammatical roles

Language	A role	S role	O role	Total
Hebrew	8% (18/232)	44%(103/232)	48% (111/232)	100% (232/232)
Sakapultek	5% (11/218)	58% (126/218)	37% (81/218)	100% (218/218)
Papago	10% (37/358)	47% (169/358)	42% (152/358)	100% (358/358)
English	8% (21/257)	35% (90/257)	57% (146/257)	100% (257/257)
Spanish	6% (35/591)	36% (215/591)	58% (341/591)	100% (591/591)
French	5% (32/646)	45% (290/646)	50% (324/646)	100% (646/646)
BrPortuguese	8%	39%	53%	100%
Japanese	7% (48/661)	48% (320/661)	44% (293/661)	100% (661/661)

One possible explanation for the scarcity of lexical As could be the scarcity of A positions that appear in the corpus. This does not appear to be the case, however. Of the 346 total clauses attested, 149 (or 43%) are transitive (or ditransitive) clauses, a fairly common proportion in oral speech.[5] Table 3.4 shows that when we take the number of lexical As as a proportion of total As, the percentage is still very low.

---

[4] The data for Sakapultek, Brazilian Portuguese, English and part of the Hebrew data are from narratives elicited from viewers of the Pear Story (Du Bois 2003a: 62–63). Du Bois does not report the exact number of tokens for Brazilian Portuguese.

[5] "Generally one-third to one-half of clauses are transitive versus two-thirds to one-half intransitive" (Du Bois 2003a: 63–64).

Table 3.4: Proportion of lexical arguments per argument position in ZAI

	A	S	O
percent lexical arguments	13% (19/149)	32% (52/165)	77% (130/168)

When viewed this way, the percentages also increase slightly for the S and O roles, but the relative proportion of each with respect to each other remains the same. That is, the PAS pattern is clear: the O role contains the highest proportion of lexical arguments, followed by the S role and finally the A role.

The ZAI data also adhere to the two quantity constraints, the One Lexical Argument constraint and the One New Argument constraint. This is illustrated in Table 3.5.

Table 3.5: Percent of transitive clauses with 0, 1, and 2 lexical arguments in ZAI

	0	1	2
percent lexical arguments	22% (33/149)	66% (98/149)	12% (18/149)

Only 18 of the 149 total transitive clauses (12%) have more than one lexical argument. There are no clauses in the corpus which contain more than one new argument.

Finally, with respect to new mentions, a new referent is introduced in A position only twice in the corpus, thus violating the Given A constraint on only two occasions. This is shown in Table 3.6:

Table 3.6: Proportion of new arguments per grammatical role in ZAI

	A	S	O
percent new arguments	1% (2/149)	11% (18/165)	21% (35/168)

In short, we have seen thus far that the ZAI data patterns as predicted by PAS: lexical and new arguments are avoided in A position and the number of clauses with more than one lexical argument or new argument are very few. Because the number of new referents introduced and the number of clauses used by each speaker will no doubt vary from speaker to speaker depending on factors such as genre or topic, one important issue related to the frequency of lexical and new As is what Du Bois terms "information pressure":

> When a number of new protagonists are introduced within the space of a few clauses, the *information pressure* is higher than when fewer protagonists are introduced in the same number of clauses-or when the same number of protagonists are introduced in a longer sequence of clauses. (Du Bois 1987: 834 (italics mine))

As Du Bois notes, the issue is especially relevant because in texts with low information pressure, few new or lexical mentions are likely in any grammatical role. Conversely, in texts with high information pressure, many new or lexical mentions are likely in any role. In this corpus, clauses with no lexical arguments are much less frequent than clauses with one lexical argument, as was shown in Table 3.5.

It is an open question, of course, whether this is a generalizable fact about ZAI narrative discourse. If we calculate the "Information Pressure Quotient" (IPQ) for the ZAI data, defined as the total number of new mentions divided by the total number of clauses, we end up with an IPQ of 0.159 (55/346). This IPQ is very similar to the one reported by Du Bois (1987: 834) for Sakapultek Maya, which translates to approximately one new introduction every 6.5 clauses. More likely, however, given the variation in the number of clauses per individual narrative (as high as 74 for one speaker and as low as 24 for another), the degree of information pressure will differ depending on factors such as the genre, the topic, and the individual speaker. We would expect a different corpus with a different degree of information pressure to show a different proportion of clauses with one or zero lexical arguments. Crucially though, due to the two Quantity constraints, we would not expect a higher proportion of clauses with two lexical or new arguments.

Based on the quantitative data reviewed thus far and summarized in Tables 3.2-3.6, it appears that ZAI speakers conform closely to the PAS constraints proposed by Du Bois. But given the amount of cross-linguistic data that has been collected in support of the same discourse tendencies (see Table 3.3 as well as the studies in Du Bois et al. (2003), this does not come as a surprise. The question I would like to pursue in the next section is: *Why?*

3.1.3 PAS and the notion of Accessibility

One of the important insights of PAS, then, has been that there is a cross-linguistic tendency for new and lexical arguments to avoid the A role and to appear most consistently in the S and O roles. Conversely, there is a tendency for old or given arguments to occur more commonly in the A and S roles.

The question of what the underlying mechanisms are that might be responsible for the PAS patterns observed cross-linguistically is formulated succinctly by Haspelmath (2006: 910). He argues that while the majority of the research supporting PAS assumes the constraints in Table 3.1 as given, few of the existing studies question whether those constraints do not ultimately reflect other, more basic linguistic and cognitive mechanisms underlying discourse.

Haspelmath points out two main issues with PAS. Most critically, he shows that there is a very close relationship between the constraints referring to lexical arguments and those referring to new arguments: *new arguments tend to be coded with full lexical forms* (a connection that was also noted by Du Bois 1987: 829–830). In Haspelmath's view, then, the four constraints could potentially be reduced to just one Quantity constraint and one Role constraint.

Second, Hasplemath raises the important question of whether the Quantity tendencies do not follow straightforwardly from the Role tendencies. That is, if speakers avoid new and/or lexical As, they automatically avoid clauses with two new or lexical core arguments, because there are maximally two core arguments (A and O). Based on this, Haspelmath (2006: 911) suggests that "it may well be that the quantity maxims can be dispensed with, that is, the universally observable quantity tendencies are reducible to whatever explains the [Given A and Non-lexical A constraints]".

So, what might explain the Given A and Non-lexical A constraints? These two constraints can arguably be based on the strong correlation between the A role, animacy and topicality. Because animates tend to be topical, and topical entities tend to be coded with non-lexical forms, the two constraints can be shown to be the result of more fundamental properties of discourse, without the need for any independent maxims.

This is one of the main impulses behind a study by Everett (2009), who takes up Haspelmath's main criticisms and argues in favor of an explanation of the deeper generalizations behind the four PAS constraints. In particular, he argues, based on data from English and Portuguese, that the inherent tendency for the A role to be dissociated with lexical and new mentions is motivated by the tendency of the A role to be filled by human referents, which are inherently more topical, and for the S and O roles to be filled by non-human referents which are less topical.

The data in Table 3.7 show that the same holds for the ZAI data, at least as far as the A and O roles are concerned.

Table 3.7: Percent human referents per core grammatical role

	A role	S role	O role
percent human	99% (147/149)	88% (146/165)	32% (53/168)

Although the percentage of human referents in the S role is very high, the point made by Everett still holds: As tend to be topical and represented anaphorically since they typically represent humans.[6] Os should tend to be new and represented more frequently by lexical arguments since they typically refer to non-humans, which are generally non-topical. Ss represent a middle ground in that they present relatively less human referents than As (and therefore more lexical and new arguments), but more than Os. In other words, for Everett, the observed patterns in the proportion of lexical As, Ss, and Os can be reduced to the factor of human-ness.[7]

Here, I build on the arguments made by Haspelmath (2006) and Everett (2009) (as well as Haig & Schnell 2016 and Brickell & Schnell 2017) and claim that the underlying reasons for the PAS patterns observed cross-linguistically are related to basic discourse-functional factors, such as topicality and animacy. In contrast to those authors, I propose a different mechanism responsible for the PAS patterns, that is, that the fundamental mechanism driving the avoidance of new and lexical As in discourse can be shown to be one of accessibility (Ariel 1990; 2001). According to the view developed here, the fact that lexical and new referents tend to correlate with grammatical roles in certain predictable ways is due to the degree of accessibility of the referents that appear in the respective grammatical roles.

In the rest of this chapter, I explore the idea that, because new referents are (almost) always coded using lexical arguments, these tendencies can be accounted for using Ariel's scalar notion of accessibility (Ariel 1990; 2001): As tend to be highly topical and hence highly accessible and thus rarely new and rarely coded with full lexical forms; Os tend to be relatively non-topical and hence inaccessible, frequently the locus of introduction for new referents, and thus often coded

---

[6]In Everett's words, "Humans like to talk about humans" (Everett 2009: 21).

[7]See also Haig & Schnell (2016) and Brickell & Schnell (2017) for further empirical, cross-linguisitic study and discussion in this direction.

using full lexical forms; Ss, frequently topical but also often the stage for new referents, form somewhat of a middle ground.

Ariel (1990; 2001)'s scalar notion of accessibility is based on the premise that a nominal expression is best characterized as an instruction for the addressee to retrieve a piece of information from either the physical world or the discourse context by indicating how accessible or salient the particular piece of information is to the addressee at that particular point in the discourse. From the perspective of accessibility, "nominal expressions are actually accessibility markers" (Ariel 2001: 31).

How do nominal expressions indicate different degrees of accessibility? Ariel (2001: 32) claims that "the more informative, rigid, and unattenuated an expression is, the lower the degree of accessibility it codes, and vice versa, the less informative, rigid, and more attenuated an expression is, the higher the degree of accessibility it codes". In other words, different nominal expressions have different discourse functions because they are marked for different degrees of accessibility: less attenuated nominal expressions such as LNPs signal less highly accessible or less salient referents, while attenuated expressions such as pronouns or zeros signal more highly accessible or more salient referents.

The possible link between Du Bois' theory of PAS and Ariel's Accessibility theory has been mentioned sporadically by the authors themselves, but to my mind has not been sufficiently developed. For example, Ariel (2001: 67) states:

> If the motivation [Du Bois] proposes for ergative and accusative markings is based on the lexical versus nonlexical distinction, then it is probably based on the consistently high degree of accessibility of agents versus the inconsistent degree of accessibility associated with intransitive subjects and objects, rather than on the given-new distinction between them.

In later work, Du Bois (2006: 194) remarks that he "started thinking about PAS in terms of accessibility theory and, more specifically, the notion of topicality or salience in terms of high versus low accessibility." To my knowledge, however, this claim has not yet been forcefully stated in the literature. No detailed studies exist which explore the possibility that the deeper generalization behind the distribution of new and lexical arguments in the A versus the S and O roles is this: accessibility and the cognitive costs associated with different types of nominal expressions.

One goal, then, is to draw a firm connection between the degree of accessibility, the forms of nominal expressions, and the three core grammatical roles, S, A, and O. In short, the link between PAS and Ariel's notion of accessibility is this: the O role tends to house low accessible referents that are coded with more linguistic material, such as LNPs. The A role tends to house highly accessible referents that are coded with less linguistic material, such as zeros. The tendencies for the S role will be found somewhere between these two poles, tending more towards the O role in the marking of new information, but more towards the A role in contexts of topic continuity, i.e. the marking of topical or human elements. Therefore, I propose that the PAS tendencies can be represented graphically in terms of accessibility in the following way:

(1) Accessibility and PAS

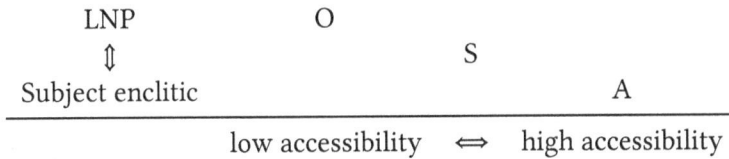

       LNP   O

        ⇕   S

   Subject enclitic   A

           low accessibility ⇔ high accessibility

Importantly, Ariel emphasizes that often more than one factor acts simultaneously to affect the degree of accessibility– and thus the form– of nominal expressions. Several of the main factors involved are listed in (2):

(2) Main factors involved in assessing the degree of accessibility[8] (Ariel 1990; 2001)

    a. Number of previous mentions, i.e. number of new vs. old mentions
    b. Grammatical role, i.e. subject versus non-subject
    c. Animacy
    d. Degree of discourse salience or topicality, i.e. topics vs. non-topics
    e. Recency of mention
    f. Paragraph and frame boundaries, i.e. paragraph-initial positions such as episode boundaries

I have already discussed several of these factors: two (number of new mentions and grammatical role) are directly mentioned in the PAS constraints, and two

---

[8] This list is not an exhaustive one. For example, Ariel (2001: 50) emphasizes the role that phonetic and intonational cues might play in marking the degree of accessibility of a referent. She mentions Mithun (1995) who shows how the same accessibility marker, a definite NP, can encode different degrees of accessibility through prosodic cues: low degrees of accessibility are encoded by definite NPs which occur in separate intonation units, slightly higher degrees of accessibility are encoded by definite NPs which are not separated by any intonational cues, and high degrees of accessibility are encoded by definite NPs that occur in the more given syntactic position (in Central Pomo) with a specific, unmarked intonation.

(animacy and topicality) are factors that have been suggested to be fundamental in motivating those constraints (Haspelmath 2006; Everett 2009). The remaining two factors (recency of mention and episode boundaries) are taken up in §3.1.6 and §3.1.8.

In the remainder of the chapter, I analyze these accessibility factors with respect to the ZAI data and show that all of the factors, subsumed under the notion of accessibility, not only condition the forms of nominal expressions but also restrict their distribution to specific grammatical roles. I explore the extent to which the gradable notion of accessibility can be shown to underlie the PAS patterns in ZAI, by asking the following questions:

- What types of accessibility markers occur in the corpus in each of the three grammatical roles?

- What are the main accessibility factors involved in determining the distribution of nominal expressions across the three roles?

- To what extent can the notion of accessibility, as a notion that encompasses at least the factors listed above in (2), sufficiently account for the patterns found in the ZAI data?

To answer these questions, each argument in the Pear Story corpus was coded for the following five factors:

(3) Coding scheme
    a. Form of reference: lexical, pronominal, or zero
    b. Core grammatical role: S, A, or O
    c. Animacy: human vs. non-human
    d. Level of salience: New, Previous subject, Active, Old (see (4) for details)
    e. Appearance at episode boundaries

This coding scheme includes each of the accessibility factors listed in (2). It is based on the coding scheme used by Arnold (2003) in her study of constraints on reference form in Mapudungan, but it differs in my formulation of the category Active (see (4) below) and in the inclusion of two categories: animacy and appearance at episode boundaries. To simplify the quantitative analysis, only matrix clauses were included in counting the number of referents that occurred in each of the three roles. Since one focus of this study is the distribution of zero versus overt third person reference forms, I did not want to include cases

where either type of mention was disallowed. A more detailed identification of
the conditions under which one or other form is used is discussed in §4. For
the purposes of the PAS study, however, subordinate and relative clauses, which
were very infrequent, were excluded. Finally, given the special nature of "presentational" or "sentence focus" constructions ("out of the blue" constructions; cf.
§6.1.1; §5.1.2) that typically appear at the beginnings of narratives, they have also
been excluded. In the majority of cases, the speakers began the narrative with a
transitive clause containing a LNP in both the A and the O role (e.g. *cuchuugube
ti rigola pera* 'A man is/was picking pears'). Since these types of constructions
were not found in other parts of the Pear Story corpus, they are excluded from
the analysis (except, of course, in the relevant sections dealing with the introduction of new referents) as they would otherwise have inaccurately biased the
data.

3.1.4 Accessibility and the introduction of new referents

In ZAI, singular indefinite referents are typically introduced using *ti* 'one' followed by a noun phrase, as in *ti xcuidi* 'INDEF + child' or *ti badunguiiu* 'INDEF +
man'. Plural indefinite referents are introduced with a quantifier such as *cadxi*
'some' as in *cadxi cuananaxhi* 'some fruit'. Referents may also be introduced as a
bare (uncountable) noun *bicicleta* 'bicycle' or within a possessor phrase such as
lari stibe 'his shirt' (cloth + POSS=3SG).

Since new referents are referents that have not previously been introduced to
the discourse, we would expect them to be referred to with the lowest accessiblity
markers, lexical NPs (LNP). This is indeed the case, as is shown in Table 3.8.

Table 3.8: Distribution of new mentions (all referents) by grammatical
role

	A role	S role	O role	Total
Lexical NP (LNP)	4% (2/55)	33% (18/55)	64% (35/55)	100% (55/55)
Dependent pronoun (DPR)	0	0	0	0
Independent pronoun (IPR)	0	0	0	0

All new referents are introduced with a lexical NP. The main tendency is for indefinite NPs of the type *ti badunguiiu* 'INDEF + man' to be used to mark previously "unidentifiable" and subsequently "activated" referents (Lambrecht 1994). This occurs in 58% (32/55) of the cases. In the remaining cases (42% (23/55)), NPs preceded by a quantifier, such as *chonna badunguiiuhuiini* 'three + boys', or bare NPs, such as *pera* 'pear', are used.

As is predicted by PAS, the majority of new referents are introduced in the O role, followed by the S role, while only two new referents in the entire corpus are introduced in the A role. This pattern is expected, as is predicted by the graphic in (1): high accessibility markers such as LNPs tend to occur in the O role while low accessibility markers such as pronouns tend to occur in the A role.

Interestingly, this pattern becomes skewed somewhat if we introduce the factor of animacy and consider only the introduction of human referents. This is shown in Table 3.9.

Table 3.9: Distribution of new mentions (human referents) by grammatical role

	A role	S role	O role	Total
LNP	7% (2/28)	54% (15/28)	39% (11/28)	100% (28/28)

When we factor in animacy, the proportion of new referents introduced in each role changes: now, the majority of new human referents are introduced in the S role, followed by the O role, and to a much lesser extent, the A role. The pattern found in Table 3.9 is due to the fact that human participants tend to be more salient and, hence, more accessible than non-human referents, which allows them to be introduced at a higher rate in the S role.

Furthermore, a referent that is introduced in the S role, as opposed to the O role, marks that referent as subsequently more accessible.[9] This is perhaps most visible when we consider the types of human referents that were introduced in each role. For example, the most salient human participant in the Pear story around whom the majority of the action occurs is the bike boy, who was introduced exclusively in the S role. Meanwhile, the least salient human participant, the Bike girl, was introduced exclusively in the O role.

---

[9]Du Bois (1987: 831) argues that the S role acts as a cognitive "staging area". I come back to this idea below.

3.1.5 Accessibility and co-reference

There are significant differences between the forms speakers use to introduce referents and the forms they use to track the referents through the narrative. Whereas new referents are always introduced using LNPs, the array of nominal forms available for coding non-new referents is wider. In this section, I present data showing that the nominal expressions ZAI speakers employ correlate with the accessibility factors of animacy, topicality, recency of mention, episode boundaries and, crucially, with grammatical role.[10] The reason that specific types of nominal forms strongly tend to occur in certain core argument positions is because they mark specific levels of accessibility. In particular, we find that low accessibility markers tend to avoid the A role and to occur most regularly in the O role, conversely, that high accessibility markers tend to avoid the O role and to occur most regularly in the A role. The S role, in contrast, tends to house high accessibility markers in contexts of topic continuity and low accessibility markers in contexts of new or marked information.

In the tracking of already-introduced referents, ZAI speakers have two basic anaphoric strategies available: lexical noun phrases (plus a demonstrative) and pronouns (see §3.1.7 for discussion). One of four demonstrative forms may appear after either a singular or a plural noun. The four-way distinction between proximal (for objects near to the speaker), mesioproximal (for objects near to the addressee), mesiodistal (for objects away from both of both speaker and addressee but rather near), and distal (for objects far away from both) demonstratives is shown in Table 3.10:

Table 3.10: ZAI demonstratives

proximal	*ri'*
mesioproximal	*ca*
mesiodistal	*rica'*
distal	*que*

Plural noun phrases are additionally marked using the plural marker *ca* as in *ca badunguiiu que* 'those boys' (PL + boy + DIST) or with a quantifier, as in *chonna badunguiiu que* 'those three boys' (three + boy + DIST).

---

[10]It is important to note, however, that although Ariel considers grammatical role a factor in accessibility marking (see (2b)), she does not make the distinction between subject of transitive verbs (A) and subjects of intransitive verbs (S). However, I believe that this distinction is critical in assessing degrees of accessibility, as we will see below.

Table 3.11 shows the distribution of each type of form per grammatical role.

Table 3.11: Frequency of forms used for co-reference: LNPs + Demonstrative vs. Pronouns

	A	S	O	Total
LNP + DEM	12% (17/146)	23% (34/146)	65% (95/146)	100% (146/146)
Pronouns	46% (130/281)	40% (113/281)	14% (38/281)	100% (281/281)

Here we see that when we exclude new referents from the count, referents encoded with LNP + Demonstrative, i.e. a low accessibility marker, still occur most often in the O role (65%) and least often in the A role (12%). Within these, the proximal form is used only twice, the medial form only once, and the distal form never. The distal demonstrative is by far the most frequent. Also, as we would also expect, referents encoded with pronouns, i.e. high accessibility markers, occur most often in the A role (46%) and least often in the O role (14%).

One additional piece of data worth commenting on here is the differential rate of lexical mention between the A and S roles that emerges in Table 3.11. It appears that transitive subjects (As) are half as likely to be coded using a LNP than are intransitive subjects (Ss). As we saw in §3.1.2, Du Bois (1987) attributes this tendency to the One Lexical Argument Constraint (the tendency to use only one lexical argument per clause). According to Du Bois, this tendency was, in turn, due to the fact that As tend to be "given" or salient more often than Ss, resulting in a lower rate of lexical reference. As Arnold (2003: 237) argues, if this were the case, that if we hold salience constant, we would expect similar rates of lexical reference for A and S. Table 3.12 appears to show that this is not the case. The categories of salience we distinguish here are (in order of low to high accessibility): New, Old, Active, and Previous Subject (further review and description of these categories will be covered in the next section, 3.1.6).

Table 3.12: Lexical arguments for A and S at each level of salience

	New	Old	Act	PrS
A	100% (2/2)	43% (6/14)	21% (5/24)	6% (6/109)
S	100% (18/18)	74% (23/31)	27% (6/22)	5% (5/94)

Here, the A role contains a significantly lower rate of lexical reference for the level of salience categorized as "Old" and a slightly lower rate for the level "Active". Therefore, when salience is held constant, LNPs are still used more for S than for A. For Arnold, this is evidence that the One Lexical Argument Constraint cannot be explained based on discourse factors such as topicality.

From the perspective of accessibility, however, this is not necessarily true. One of the reasons that the high rate of lexical arguments in the S role in "Old" contexts is that more than 40% (10 out of 23) of the tokens are used to refer to non-human referents. In contrast, only 17% (1 out of 6) of the lexical arguments in the A role in "Old" contexts are used to refer to non-human referents. The data in Table 3.12 thus ignore the tendency for human referents to be more salient and, therefore, more likely to be transitive agents (i.e. the *potentiality of agency scale* Silverstein (1976) than non-human referents. For this reason, I suspect that the different rates of lexical arguments for S than for A are not due to the One Lexical Argument Constraint, as Arnold (2003) claims, but to the independent tendency for the A role to house human, highly salient and, therefore, highly accessible referents.

At this point, it should be clear from this discussion as well as from Table 3.7 (§3.1.3) and Table 3.9 (§3.1.4) that animacy strongly influences accessibility and, hence, the distribution of nominal expressions per grammatical role. In what follows, I examine the categories of full lexical noun phrases (LNP) and pronouns in more detail with respect to two additional accessibility factors, topicality and recency of mention (both captured under the label 'salience').

3.1.6 LNPs and salience

We would expect the two accessibility factors of topicality and recency of mention to correlate in predictable ways with the occurrence of LNPs. The effects of these two factors in the ZAI data can be observed through the use of the coding scheme for salience described in (4).

I use the term salience here in the same sense as Arnold (2003) since it effectively combines two of the factors in (2), recency of mention and topicality. The result is a four level scale:

(4) Salience of discourse referents (adapted from Arnold 2003: 231)

    New = New: referent is brand new to the text.

    Old = Old: referent had appeared previously in the text, but not in the previous three clauses.

Act = Active: referent was last mentioned as either the object of the previous three clauses, as a subpart of the subject or object in the previous three clauses, or both subject and object of the previous three clauses together.[11]

PrS = Previous subject: referent mentioned as subject of the previous clause.

This scheme allows us to observe how referential forms can be simultaneously affected by several discourse constraints. In particular, distinguishing between these four levels in this way allows us to measure differences in salience between both recency of mention (by comparing "Previous Subject" with "Active" and "Old") and topicality (by comparing "Previous Subject" with "Active"). I thus assume salience to be a gradable scale (Hopper & Thompson 1980) – where referents can be more or less salient– and for the relative values on this scale to coincide directly with those on the scale of accessibility – where referents can be more or less accessible.

First, with respect to recency of mention, reference to something in the previous three clauses ("PrS" and "Act") is less likely to be encoded with a LNP than reference to something prior to those three clauses ("New" and "Old"). This is shown in Table 3.13.

Table 3.13: Percent of LNPs and recency of mention

Reference to:	% lexical
Entities in the previous clause or previous three clauses (PrS + Act)	26% (53/201)
Entities prior to three clauses (New + Old)	74% (148/201)

Of all the LNPs in the corpus, three times as many occurred in "New" and "Old" contexts than in "PrS" and "Act" contexts. In other words, more recent mentions are less likely to be coded with a LNP than are less recent mentions.

Second, with respect to topicality, reference to a subject (A or S) in the previous clause or in the previous three clauses (PrS) is less likely to be encoded with a LNP

---

[11] This category allows for the distinction between the relative discourse prominence of an antecedent that was mentioned in subject position and an antecedent that was mentioned in a non-subject position (Arnold 2003: 226). I have decided to adjust this category slightly from Arnold (2003: 231)'s formulation to include the previous three clauses (and not only the previous clause), because I think it more accurately describes the patterns observed in the data, particularly the distribution of pronouns and demonstratives.

than reference to a non-subject in any of the previous three clauses (Act). This is shown in Table 3.14. Of the LNPs in the corpus, three times as many occurred

Table 3.14: Percent of LNPs and topicality

Reference to:	% lexical
Subject (A or S) of the previous clause or previous three clauses (PrS)	28% (15/53)
Non-subject in any of the previous three clauses (Act)	72% (38/53)

in "Act" contexts than in "PrS" contexts. That is, more topical referents are less likely to be coded with a LNP than are less topical referents.

Based on these correlations as well as those we have set up between low degrees of accessibility, LNPs and the O role on one hand and high degrees of accessibility, pronouns and the A role on the other, we would expect recency of mention and topicality to also correlate with grammatical role in the following way: referents that occur in the O role will be less topical and less recent (and coded as "New" or "Old") while referents that occur the A role will be more topical and recent (and coded as "Previous Subject"). Table 3.15 shows that this pattern indeed holds for the ZAI data.

Table 3.15: Frequency of referents in each category of salience

	A	S	O
New	1% (2/149)	11% (18/165)	21% (35/168)
Old	9% (14/149)	19% (31/165)	44% (74/168)
Act	16% (24/149)	13% (22/165)	30% (50/168)
PrS	74% (109/149)	57% (94/165)	5% (9/168)
Total	100% (149/149)	100% (165/165)	100% (168/168)

Conversely, we would also expect the majority of less topical and less recent arguments, such as those found in "New" and "Old" contexts, to occur in the O role and for the majority of more topical and more recent arguments, such as those found in "Previous Subject" contexts, to occur in the A role. This is also what we find, as shown in Table 3.16. The A role appears specialized for more topical and more recent mentions, while the O role is more specialized for mentions that are less topical and less recent.

Table 3.16: Frequency of referents in each category of salience

	A	S	O	Total
New	4% (2/55)	33% (18/55)	63% (35/55)	100% (55/55)
Old	12% (14/119)	26% (31/119)	62% (74/119)	100% (119/119)
Act	25% (24/96)	23% (22/96)	52% (50/96)	100% (96/96)
PrS	51% (109/212)	44% (94/212)	5% (9/212)	100% (212/212)

Finally, we would predict the tendencies shown in Tables 3.15 and 3.16 to correlate with particular types of nominal expressions. That is, we would predict low accessibility markers such as LNPs to occur most often in contexts categorized as "New" and "Old" and high accessibility markers such as pronouns to occur most often in "Previous Subject" contexts. As Table 3.17 shows, this is also what we find.

Table 3.17: Type of nominal expression per category of salience

	New	Old	Act	PrS
LNP + DEM	100% (55/55)	88% (93/106)	53% (38/68)	7% (15/202)
Pronouns	0% (0/55)	12% (13/106)	47% (30/68)	93% (187/202)
Total	100% (55/55)	100% (106/106)	100% (68/68)	100% (202/202)

The inverse relation that exists between degrees of salience (defined in terms of topicality and recency of mention) and rates of LNPs should be clear: a high degree of salience and accessibility correlates with a low rate of LNPs and a low degree of salience and accessibility correlates with a high rate of LNPs. Further, the relation should also be clear between high rates of LNPs and the O role as well as low rates of LNPs and the A role. In the next section, I analyze the relation between degrees of salience and the distribution of higher accessibility expressions, i.e. pronouns.

3.1.7 Pronouns and salience

The ZAI pronominal system is summarized in Table 3.18. This system does not distinguish between masculine and feminine, or between formal and informal. The third person pronoun differentiates between human, animal, and inanimate. In addition, first person plural distinguishes between inclusive and exclusive.

Table 3.18: The ZAI pronominal system

	Dependent form	Independent form
1SG	*-a'*	*naa*
2SG	*-lu'*	*lii*
3SG.HUM	*-be, -∅*	*laa-be, laa-∅*
3SG.ANIM	*-me, -∅*	*laa-me, laa-∅*
3SG.INAN	*-ni, -∅*	*laa-ni, ni, laa-∅*
1PL.INCL	*-nu*	*laa-nu*
1PL.EXCL	*-du*	*laa-du*
2PL	*-tu*	*laa-tu*
3PL.HUM	*-ca-be, -ca-∅*	*laa-ca-be, laa-ca-∅*
3PL.ANIM	*-ca-me, -ca-∅*	*laa-ca-me, laa-ca-∅*
3PL.INAN	*-ca-ni, -ca-∅*	*laa-ca-ni, -cani, laa-ca-∅*

Although NPs are not marked for case in ZAI, pronouns do have independent and dependent forms that are sensitive to their grammatical position within the clause. Dependent forms occur immediately after the verb or noun. In all other positions, the independent form is used which is comprised of a base form *laa* plus the dependent pronoun. For example, the third person singular pronoun can be realized as an overt form or as a zero form and, when used in object position, before the verb, or in isolation, the pronoun base *laa* carries the dependent pronoun.[12] The dependent forms mark already activated referents, i.e. they mark continuing topics. These forms do not mark the same contrasts as the independent forms, which can function as either topical or focal expressions. In a canonical verb-inital clause, pronouns in the S and A roles appear in the dependent form as enclitics on the verb. Pronouns in the O role occur in the independent form after the subject.

In the remainder of this section, I focus on two main distinctions that appear in (3.1.7). First, I compare the distribution in the Pear Story corpus of the overt third-person singular dependent form, *=be*, to that of the zero form, *=∅*. Second, I analyze the distribution of dependent pronouns versus independent pronouns.

---

[12] The option to use an independent form for the A or S role, as in the case of "marked topics", does exist. These cases will be discussed in more detail below.

3.1.7.1 Distribution of third-person dependent pronouns: overt vs. zero

In simple intransitive (5 – 6) or simple transitive constructions (7 – 8), the choice between the overt or the zero form of the pronominal subject clitic is free (Marlett & Pickett 1996):

(5) biababe   láyu
    bi-aba=be^{LH} layu
    COMPL-fall=3SG ground
    'S/he fell on the ground.'

(6) biaba   layu
    bi-aba=∅   layú
    COMPL-fall=3SG ground
    'S/he fell on the ground.'

(7) biiyabe   bá'du quě
    bi-iya=be^{LH} ba'du' que^{LH}
    COMPL-see=3SG child   DIST
    'S/he saw the child.'

(8) biiya   ba'du quě
    bi-iya=∅   ba'du' que^{LH}
    COMPL-see=3SG child   DIST
    'S/he saw the child.'

The intransitive clauses in (5) and (6) convey the same propositional content. However, whereas in (5) the S role is occupied by the overt third person pronoun =*be*, in (6) the S role is occupied by the zero form. This alternation is possible in transitive clauses as well, as is shown in (7), which contains the overt form, and (8), which contains the zero form.

If the choice between the two forms is indeed free at the level of the main clause, it is important to consider the discourse conditions are under which each of the two forms is used. One possibility is that the distribution of the forms is conditioned by grammatical role. This possibility is explored in Table 3.19.

What emerges from this table is a strong preference for overt marking. However, although there may be a slight preference for the overt form to appear in the A role, there does not seem to be a significant difference between the two forms in the grammatical role with which they are associated.

Table 3.19: Frequency of third-person singular overt vs. zero DPR per grammatical role

	A	S
=*bě*	78% (73/93)	73 % (58/79)
=∅	22% (20/93)	27% (21/79)
Total	100% (93/93)	100% (79/79)

Table 3.20: Frequency of third-person singular overt vs. zero for each level of salience

	New	Old	Act	PrS
=*bě*	0	73% (8/11)	90% (18/20)	74% (106/144)
=∅	0	27% (3/11)	10% (2/20)	26% (38/144)
Total	0	100% (11/11)	100% (20/20)	100% (144/144)

A second possibility is that the distribution of the overt versus the zero form correlates with one or more levels of salience. This is represented in Table 3.20.

These data show that zero forms are much more restricted in terms of the degree of salience compared to the overt forms. That is, while overt pronouns may occur somewhat freely at each level of salience (except, of course, for "New"), zero pronouns appear to be much more restricted to "PrS" contexts– there are only five total uses of the zero form outside of "PrS" contexts.

Here for "Old" and "PrS" the distribution is very similar to Table 3.19 (in PrS it is basically identical). Only the numbers reported for "Act" stand out. This pattern would appear to imply that topicality and not recency of mention is the crucial factor in whether the zero form is employed. That is, the use of the zero form, higher on the accessibility scale than the overt form, is restricted to highly topical referents, whereas the overt form may be used for either highly topical or recently mentioned referents. For the purposes of this section, I leave this question unresolved for now and return to it in Chapter 4, where I argue that the distribution of the two forms is related to a distinction between primary and secondary topic.

3.1.7.2 Independent pronouns in the A or S role

While the most common way to refer to subjects in the A or S role is through the use of dependent pronouns, it is also possible in ZAI to use an independent pronoun in pre-verbal position. These are cases that Du Bois terms "marked topics": "NPs which are topicalized and set off in a separate intonation unit without a verb, and usually precede a predication about the same referent in the immediately following clausal intonation unit" (Du Bois 1987: 814, note 11).[13] In the ZAI data, there are 25 instances in which an independent pronoun is used in this way. Consider the following example:

(9) 01 biabandabě

bi-abanda=be^{LH}

COMPL-fall.hard=3SG

'He fell.'

02 birěeche   dxúmí   pěrá   stí=bě

bi-ree^{LH}che^{LH} dxumi^{LH} pe^{LH}ra sti^{LH}=be^{LH}

COMPL-spill   basket   pear   POSS-3SG

'His basket of pears spilled.'

03 **laabe**   lá,

laa=be^{LH} la^{H}

BASE=3SG LA

'As for him,'

04 biiyadxisibé   bádudxaapahuiini quě

bi-iyadxisi^{LH}=be^{LH} badudxaapa-huiini que^{LH}

COMPL-see.fixedly=3SG girl-DIM   DIST

'He looked fixedly at the little girl.'

Here, the subject of the intransitive verb in the first intonation unit is the bike boy and the subject of the intransitive verb in the second intonation unit is the basket of pears. In the immediately following intonation unit, line 3, the third person singular independent pronoun is used to refer to the bike boy, followed by the particle LA.[14] The marked topic in the third line therefore helps to signal

---

[13]Importantly, for the purposes of coding the data, marked topics were treated as one mention (of an independent pronoun), not two mentions (one independent pronoun plus one dependent pronoun).

[14]The LA particle always appears at the end of an intonation unit. It appears in 23 of the 25 tokens in which the marked topic strategy is used. It also appears consistently at the end when-clauses and if-clauses. One possibility, then, is that it is used as a topic or contrastive topic marker. This issue will be taken up again in §6.2.

the change in subject from the basket back to the bike boy. The last intonation unit, line 4, consists of a transitive clause in which the A role is filled by the third person singular pronoun *=be* and the O role by a LNP that refers to the girl. Of the 25 instances in which this strategy is used in the corpus, 20 (or 80%) signal a change in subject from the previous sentence.

Contrastive forms such as these are generally used in contexts where there is a switch in subject from the previous sentence because they signal referents that are not predicted to occur in particular roles. The account sketched here based on accessibility in fact predicts this to be the case. Ariel (2001: 37) states that, "when an entity is not predicted to appear in a certain role, its degree of accessibility is (relatively) low." In other words, despite having the exact same form, marked topics with topicalized IPRs indicate a lower degree of accessibility (i.e. they signal a change in subject) than do IPRs in their more common O role position.

To this point, I have tried to show that there exists a strong correlation in the ZAI data between nominal expressions such as LNPs, overt and zero dependent pronouns, and independent pronouns on the one hand, and certain grammatical roles (S, A, or O) on the other. Further, I have argued that the reasons for the strong correlation can be traced to different degrees of salience that are associated with the grammatical roles in which the nominal expressions are used. Overt and zero dependent pronouns are preferred over LNPs in the S and A roles because those roles tend to house more salient referents. In contrast, independent pronouns and LNPs are preferred in the O role because of the tendency for the O role to house less salient referents. In the next section, I conclude this analysis by looking closely at one additional factor involved in the distribution of these nominal expressions across grammatical roles: episode boundaries.

3.1.8 Episode boundaries

Do speakers use different nominal forms according to different episode boundaries? We can distinguish five main episode boundaries that each of the speakers marked in their narratives about the Pear film. These are listed in (10):

(10)   Five episode boundaries
1.   The Pear man is picking pears.
2.   The Bike boy passes by on his bike and steals a basket of pears.
3.   The Bike boy passes the Bike girl, hits a rock and falls.
4.   Three boys appear and help the boy get up and pick up the pears that spilled.
5.   The Three boys walk away, passing the Pear man by the pear tree

Out of the 35 episode boundaries in the seven narratives, 16 were marked with an intransitive clause and 19 with a transitive clause.

Since low accessibility markers regularly occur in paragraph-initial positions such as episode boundaries (Ariel 2001: 52), we would expect clauses at episode boundaries to contain higher proportions of LNPs in the A and S roles than throughout the rest of the narratives. This is in fact the case. In Table 3.21, we see that the majority of the arguments (75%) that appear in the S role at episode boundaries are coded with a LNP.

Table 3.21: Lexical arguments at episode boundaries, intransitive clauses

new lexical S	75% (12/16)
non-new lexical S	0
non lexical S	25% (4/16)

More significantly, all of the LNPs that occur in the S role at episode boundaries introduce new referents. Moreover, of the 18 total new LNPs introduced in S position in the entire corpus, 12 (or 67%) occur at episode boundaries. This conforms to the observation by Du Bois (1987: 831) that the S position acts as a cognitive "staging area" for the introduction of referents that are later tracked through combinations of transitive and intransitive clauses.

We also see a higher percentage of LNPs in transitive clauses at episode boundaries. This is shown in Table 3.22.

Table 3.22: Lexical arguments at episode boundaries, transitive clauses

	new lexical A	non-new lexical A	non-lexical A
new lexical O	0	1	11
non-new lexical O	1	4	1
non lexical O	1	0	0

LNPs occur at a much lower rate in the A role than in the S role, even at episode boundaries. However, 7 of the 19 total As at episode boundaries are LNPs. This percentage (37%) is much higher than the percentage of lexical As found overall. In addition, it is interesting to note that of the two new lexical As that appear in the entire corpus, both occur at episode boundaries.

In summary, LNPs in the A and S roles occur at a much higher rate at episode boundaries than they do at other parts of the narratives. I propose that the reason for this pattern can be also explained in terms of accessibility: episode boundaries are cross-linguistically very common sites for the occurrence of low accessibility markers (Ariel 2001: 52; see also Downing 1980).

3.1.9 Summary

The ZAI data patterns as predicted by PAS: lexical and new arguments are avoided in A position and the number of clauses with more than one lexical or new argument is extremely rare. The question this chapter has been concerned with is: *Why?* Why should the four PAS constraints hold in ZAI, as well as cross-linguistically? How are they to be explained? Are the constraints discursively motivated? If so, what are these motivations?

Other researchers (e.g. Haspelmath 2006; Everett 2009; Haig & Schnell 2016; Brickell & Schnell 2017) have pointed out, however, that the cross-linguistic tendency to observe these constraints may in fact be due to more fundamental generalizations about the nature of discourse. Three main observations stand out. First, there is a well-established correlation between human, topical referents and the A role in transitive clauses. Second, cross-linguistically what lexical arguments have in common with new arguments is that it is precisely full lexical forms that are used to introduce and track less-accessible (Ariel 1990) referents, i.e. new information. This conforms to the more general observation in the literature that the use of more coding material, i.e. fuller nominal forms, correlates strongly with referents that are lower on the accessibility scale (Givón 1983).

This chapter has presented discourse data from ZAI and has argued, in line with Haspelmath (2006), Everett (2009), Haig & Schnell (2016), and Brickell & Schnell (2017) that the constraints on new arguments and new As can be viewed as a subset of the constraints on lexical arguments and lexical As. I have proposed that the fundamental mechanism driving the tendencies captured by PAS can be traced to the notion of accessibility (Ariel 1990; 2001). This mechanism may be summarized as a reduction of the four PAS constraints to a single constraint that refers directly to the accessibility of referents in the A role: *Avoid low-accessible As.* In other words, the avoidance of new referents and LNPs in the A role can be understood as an avoidance of referents with a low degree of accessibility in that role. That this should be the case is natural given the factors involved in determining a referent's accessibility (as listed above in (2)): newly mentioned vs. already mentioned, non-subject vs. subject, animacy, topicality, recency of mention, and episode boundaries.

Highly accessible referents are referents that have already been mentioned, subjects, animate, topical, recently mentioned, and/or that do not tend to appear at episode boundaries. These are represented with relatively little *coding material* (Givón 1983). In contrast, low accessible referents are referents that are new mentions, non-subjects, inanimate, non-topical, not recently mentioned, and/or that tend to appear at episode boundaries. These are represented with relatively more coding material. Most significantly, this correlates with grammatical role: while highly accessible referents are very likely to occur in the A role, low accessible referents are very *unlikely* to occur in the A role. The correlations between accessibility factors, nominal expressions and grammatical role are summarized in Table 3.23.

Table 3.23: Accessibility scale for ZAI nominal expressions

	low accessibility	high accessibility
accessibility factors	newly mentioned non-subject inanimate non-topical not mentioned recently at episode boundary	already mentioned subject animate topical recently mentioned not at episode boundary
type of referring expression	INDEF + LNP > LNP + DEM > IPR > overt DPR > zero	
grammatical role	O S A	

These patterns are corroborated in the ZAI data presented above. On the one hand, new and/or lexical arguments are low on the accessibility scale and tend to be referred to using the forms 'INDEF + LNP' and 'LNP + DEM'. These occur most commonly in the O role. On the other hand, already introduced referents are high on the accessibility scale and tend to be referred to using more attenuated pronominal forms. These occur most commonly in the S or A role.

Interestingly, independent pronouns occupy a kind of middle ground, since they are usually used to refer to objects which tend to be less accessible than subjects, but, as in the case of "marked topics", they can also be used to refer to subjects that are relatively less accessible, i.e. subjects that are not particularly salient at a certain moment in the discourse and/or subjects that occur at episode boundaries. The function of this construction in these cases is one of topic promotion (this construction will be an important part of the discussion of topic relations in §6).

Similarly, the S role also has an intermediate function between the O and A role. The S role will often house previously mentioned, animate, salient, topical, and recent referents but, as we saw, it also frequently functions as a "cognitive staging area" for the introduction of new referents at episode boundaries.

In the next section, I move away from the analysis of Preferred Argument Structure and accessibility to examine the relationship between nominal forms and the pragmatic status of referents.

3.2 Nominal forms and the pragmatic status of referents

As we have seen throughout the course of this chapter, the forms of nominal expressions that speakers use depend on the assumed cognitive status of the referents, that is, on assumptions that a speaker can reasonably make regarding the addressee's knowledge and attention state in the specific context in which nominal expressions are used (cf. Chafe 1976; Prince 1981; Ariel 1988; *inter alia*). Certain correlations therefore hold in ZAI between the formal category and the pragmatic status of the referents such that the lexical form of an NP may convey either: 1) a request to the hearer to act as if the NP were already pragmatically available or "given", albeit to varying degrees, or 2) a request to the hearer to act as if the NP constitutes unavailable or "new" information. The various nominal forms in ZAI, namely independent and dependent pronouns, demonstratives and indefinite articles, indicate the status of their denotations as more or less activated in the speaker/hearer's mind, the discourse, or some real or possible world.[15]

Gundel et al. (1993) propose six cognitive (memory and attention) statuses relevant to the form of nominal expressions in discourse, which are implicationally related such that each status entails (and is therefore included by) all lower statuses, but not vice versa. The statuses that an entity mentioned in a sentence may have in the mind of the addressee and their relation to each other is represented in the Givenness Hierarchy in Table 3.24:

Table 3.24: Givenness Hierarchy (Gundel et. al.1993)

in focus > activated > familiar > uniquely identifiable > referential > type identifiable

---

[15] "Depending on where the referents or corresponding meanings of these linguistic expressions are assumed to reside" (Gundel & Fretheim 2001: 177).

Each status on the hierarchy is a necessary and sufficient condition for the appropriate use of a different form or forms. In using a particular form, a speaker signals that s/he assumes the associated cognitive status is met and, since each status entails all lower statuses, s/he also signals that all lower statuses (the statuses to the right) have been met (Gundel et al. 1993: 275). For example, anything in focus is also activated, anything activated is also familiar, and so on, but something that is familiar is not necessarily activated or in focus. The statuses are therefore ordered from most restrictive (in focus) to least restrictive (type identifiable), with respect to the set of possible referents they include. These are summarized in (11):

(11)   Six cognitive statuses proposed by Gundel et al. (1993)

- *Type identifiable.* The addressee is able to access a representation of the type of object described by the expression.
- *Referential.* The addressee not only needs to access an appropriate type-representation, s/he must either retrieve an existing representation of the speaker's intended referent or construct a new representation by the time the sentence has been processed.
- *Uniquely identifiable.* In contrast to expressions which are referential but not uniquely identifiable, expressions which are both referential and uniquely identifiable require the addressee to construct or retrieve a representation on the basis of the nominal expression alone. Identifiability may be based on an already existing representation in the addressee's memory.
- *Familiar.* The addressee is able to uniquely identify the intended referent because he already has a representation of it in memory (in long-term memory if it has not been recently mentioned or perceived, or in short-term memory if it has).
- *Activated.* The referent is represented in current short-term memory. Activated representations may have been retrieved from long-term memory, or they may arise from the immediate linguistic or extralinguistic context. They therefore always include the speech participants themselves.
- *In focus.* The referent is not only in short-term memory, but is also at the current center of attention. Entities in focus generally include at least the topic of the preceding utterance, as well as any still-relevant higher-order topics.

The forms that encode statuses on the Givenness Hierarchy thus provide procedural information about the manner of cognitive accessibility (or accessibility of representations of the intended referent) and thereby guide the addressee in restricting possible interpretations to ones whose status is explicitly indicated by particular forms. Furthermore, these hierarchical relations predict that a particular form will be inappropriate if the required cognitive status is not met.

Table 3.25 shows the correlations between pragmatic status and nominal forms in ZAI.[16]

Table 3.25: Correlations between linguistic form and pragmatic status in ZAI

In focus	Activated	Familiar	Uniquely identifiable	Referential	Type identifiable
=*bě*	independent		NP + DIST		*ti* NP 'a NP'
=∅	pronoun				∅ N
	NP + DEM				

Zero pronouns require that the referents be "in focus" while both dependent and independent pronouns require that referents be at least familiar. Indefinite NPs, in contrast, may require only that referents be type identifiable.

The four-way distinction in demonstratives (proximal, mesioproximal, mesiodistal and distal) summarized in Table 3.10 is relevant here as well. As we saw, important differences occur in the Pear Story corpus with respect to how each demonstrative is used anaphorically to refer to already introduced referents. Of the 147 lexical NPs + DEM used this way, the proximal form *ri'* is used only twice, the mesioproximal form *ca* only once and the mesiodistal form *rica'* not at all. The distal demonstrative *que* is by far the most frequent, having been employed in the remaining 144 cases. What is interesting is that the few uses of the proximate and the mesioproximal demonstratives are limited to cases in which the lexical NP refers anaphorically to a referent mentioned within the previous three clauses, i.e more familiar or more activated referents.

The above cognitive statuses generally correlate formally with type of nominal expression. As was shown, these statuses also have correlates in syntax, in par-

---

[16] Note that, based on further cross-linguistic investigation, Gundel et al. (2010) claim that: 1) if a language encodes the distinction between two adjacent statuses on the Givenness Hierarchy, it will also encode distinctions between higher statuses, and 2) all languages encode distinctions between the two highest statuses, 'in focus' and 'activated'.

ticular, with the grammatical roles of core arguments. In short, the O role tends to house less activated or 'new' referents that are coded with more linguistic material such as Lexical NPs. The A role tends to house referents that are in focus (in the sense of Gundel et al. 1993) and that are coded with less linguistic material such as zeros. The tendencies for the S role are found somewhere between these two poles, tending more towards the O role in the marking of new information, but more towards the A role in contexts of topic continuity, i.e. the marking of topical or human elements.

Finally, the cognitive status "in focus" has also been claimed to have prosodic correlates, i.e. phonological attenuation (Gundel et al. 1993: 285; but see also the cognitive category "activeness" in Lambrecht 1994; Ariel 1990; 2001). As mentioned in §2.2.4 and discussed in more detail in §5, such correlates do not exist in ZAI, at least in the form of pitch accent. In this, it may be important to consider that, in Lambrecht's words:

> "While it is true that the referent of a pronominal expression or of a nominal expression spoken with attenuated pronunciation is always taken to be active..., it is NOT the case that an expression coding a referent which is assumed to be active is necessarily also spoken with attenuated pronunciation. In other words, weak prosodic manifestation is only a sufficient, not a necessary condition for assumed activeness of a discourse referent" (Lambrecht 1994: 97; EMPHASIS in original).

For Lambrecht, then, the link between attenuated pronunciation and/or pronominal marking and highly activated referents represents the unmarked or default case whereas, in more "marked" environments, these same referents may receive emphatic pronunciation and be coded using fuller nominal forms.

Similarly, Ariel (2001: 50) emphasizes the role that phonetic and intonational cues might play in marking the degree of accessibility of a referent. She cites Mithun (1995) who shows how the same accessibility marker, a definite NP, can encode different degrees of accessibility through prosodic cues: low degrees of accessibility are encoded by definite NPs which occur in separate intonation units, slightly higher degrees of accessibility are encoded by definite NPs which are not separated by any intonational cues, and high degrees of accessibility are encoded by definite NPs that occur in the more given syntactic position (in Central Pomo) with a specific, unmarked intonation.

In the next chapter, I leave behind the relation between grammatical role, accessibility and pragmatic status, which I will come back to in §6, and I continue with the analysis of ZAI nominal forms by focusing on the alternation and distribution of overt and zero third-person clitics that was mentioned in §3.1.7.

3.3 Summary and conclusions

This chapter explored the relationship in ZAI between form and distribution of nominals by function, focusing on the ways that the different forms are used to introduce and track referents and to mark referents as more or less accessible. Through the lens of Preferred Argument Structure (Du Bois 2003a) and the theory of Accessibility (Ariel 2001), the chapter argued that the fundamental mechanism driving the PAS tendencies can be traced to the notion of accessibility.

More specifically, one of the tendencies identified by PAS, the avoidance of new referents and lexical NPs in the A role, was understood as an avoidance of referents in the A role with a low degree of accessibility. More directly, the tendency is: *Avoid low accessible As.* This is because, as we saw, highly accessible referents with less coding material are more likely to occur in the A role. In contrast, low accessible referents with characteristically more coding material are unlikely to occur in that role and more consistently occur in the O role instead. The S role, for its part, exhibits a tendency in between the A and O roles. On the one hand, it can house previously mentioned, animate, salient, topical, and recent referents. On the other hand, it can house new referents at episode boundaries, thereby functioning as a "cognitive staging area" (cf. §3.1.8).

In summary, the A role tends to house referents that are 'in focus' (Gundel et al. 1993) and coded with less linguistic material, and the O role houses referents that are less activated or "new" and coded with more linguistic material. The S role tends more towards the O role in contexts of marking new information and more towards A role in contexts of topic continuity.

Furthermore, we saw that there is a relation between the grammatical role of core arguments, accessibility, and cognitive or pragmatic status. In other words, cognitive status correlates with type of nominal expression, as well as with the grammatical roles of core arguments. These correlations were summarized in Table 3.25. This occurs because nominal forms indicate the status of their denotations as more or less activated in the speaker or hearer's mind, as pragmatically more or less available, such that the forms of nominals that speakers use depend on the assumed cognitive status of the referents involved. That is, nominal forms depend on assumptions that a speaker can reasonably make regarding the addressee's knowledge and attention state in the specific context in which the form is used.

4 Nominal forms in discourse: the alternation of third-person singular pronouns

As mentioned previously in §3.1.7, Table 3.18, third-person dependent and independent pronouns both alternate between an overt form (=*be*) and a zero form (=∅). Because the choice between the overt and the zero form is free at the main clause level in both transitive and intransitive constructions, an explanation of the differential distribution between the two requires a more detailed syntactic and pragmatic analysis. This is the subject of this section, which begins with a discussion of the syntactic facts constraining the distribution of either pronominal form and then moves to an analysis of the discursive motivations involved in their use. In order to offer a more complete view, in addition to the Pear Story corpus, the analysis here also draws from previously published studies, from data collected using elicitation techniques, and from spontaneous dialogue.

4.1 Syntactic constraints on the overt versus zero alternation

The zero form has a more constrained syntactic distribution than the overt form, that is, the zero form has a narrower set of binding conditions. This can be observed in the case of reflexives and dependent clauses.

4.1.1 Reflexives

The reflexive consists of the word *laaca* 'same' followed by an independent pronoun co-indexed with its antecedent. The zero pronoun is bound by a full NP antecedent (1) or another zero pronoun (2):

(1) biiya   Bĕtu₁   laaca   láa₁
     bi=uuya   Be^LHtu laaca^LH laa=∅
     COMPL=see Betu   SAME   BASE=3
     'Betu saw himself.'

(2) biiya₁   laaca   láa₁
     bi=uuya=∅   laaca^LH laa=∅
     COMPL=see=3 SAME   BASE=3
     'S/he saw himself/herself.'

Meanwhile, the overt pronoun can only be bound by another overt pronoun, as shown in (3)-(5):

(3) biiyabe₁   láacá   láabĕ₁
     bi=uuya=be^LH   laaca^LH laa=be^LH
     COMPL=see=3.HUM SAME   BASE=3.HUM
     'S/he saw himself/herself.'

(4) biiya   Bĕtu₁   (*laaca)   laabĕ₁
     bi=uuya   Be^LHtu (laaca^LH) laa=be^LH
     COMPL=see Betu   (SAME)   BASE=3.HUM
     'Betu saw him/her (*himself).'

(5) biiya₂   (*laaca)   laabĕ₁
     bi=uuya=∅   (laaca^LH) laa=be^LH
     COMPL=see=3 (SAME)   BASE=3.HUM
     'S/he saw him/her (*himself).'

Therefore, the overt form can only co-refer with another overt form and a zero form can co-refer with either a full NP or a zero form, but not an overt form, within the main clause. A similar situation holds for dependent clauses.

4.1.2 Dependent clauses

An overt third-person pronominal subject in a dependent clause cannot co-refer to the subject NP in the main clause:

(6) racaladxi   Bĕtu$_2$ guéedábé$_1$ íxí'
     ri=aca-ladxi   Be^{LH}tu gu^{LH}=eeda^{LH}=be^{LH} guixi'^{H}
     HAB=occur-gut Betu   POT=come=3.HUM   tomorrow
     'Betu wants him/her to come tomorrow.'   (MP 13)[1]

The overt form in the dependent clause cannot refer to Betu. Instead, a zero form must be used (7):

(7) racaladxi   Bĕtu$_1$ guéedá$_1$ íxí'
     ri=aca-ladxi   Betu gu^{LH}=eeda^{LH}=Ø guixi'^{H}
     HAB=occur-gut Betu POT=come=3   tomorrow
     'Betu wants to come tomorrow.'   (MP 22)

Identical pronominal forms obligatorily co-refer across dependent clauses, as in (8), (9):

(8) racaladxibe$_1$ guéedábé$_1$ íxí'
     ri=aca-ladxi=be^{LH} gu^{LH}=eeda^{LH}=be^{LH} guixi'^{H}
     HAB=occur-gut=3.HUM POT=come=3.HUM   tomorrow
     'S/he wants to come tomorrow.'

(9) racaladxi$_1$ guéedá$_1$ íxí'
     ri=aca-ladxi=Ø   gu=eeda^{LH}=Ø guixi'^{H}
     HAB=occur-gut=3 POT=come=3   tomorrow
     'S/he wants to come tomorrow.'

They may both either be overt or both zero. In contrast, non-identical pronominal forms do not co-refer, as shown in (10), (11):

(10) racaladxibe$_1$ guéedá$_2$ íxí'
     ri=aca-ladxi=be^{LH} gu^{LH}=eeda^{LH}=Ø guixi'^{H}
     HAB=occur-gut=3.HUM POT=come=3   tomorrow
     'S/he wants him/her to come tomorrow.'   (MP 34)

(11) racaladxi$_2$ guéedábé$_1$ íxí'
     ri=aca-ladxi=Ø   gu^{LH}=eeda^{LH}=be^{LH} guixi'^{H}
     HAB=occur-gut=3 POT=come=3.HUM   tomorrow
     'S/he wants him/her to come tomorrow.'   (MP 77)

---

[1]If the example is not from my own corpus, I refer to the source of the examples using the following notation: MP= Marlett & Pickett (1996). The number that follows refers to the example number in the source.

Similarly, an overt third-person pronominal object in a dependent clause cannot co-refer to a previously mentioned NP in the main clause (12):

(12) na Bĕtu$_1$ Yĕrmo$_2$ biiya   laabĕ$_3$
      na Be^{LH}tu Ye^{LH}rmo bi=uuya   laa=be^{LH}
      say Betu   Yermo   COMPL=see BASE=3.HUM
      'Betu$_x$ said Yermo$_y$ saw him.$_{*x,*y,z}$'   (MP 63)

The zero form must be used for co-reference (13)

(13) na Bĕtu$_1$ Yĕrmo$_2$ biiya   laa$_1$
      na Be^{LH}tu Ye^{LH}rmo bi=uuya   laa=∅
      say Betu   Yermo   COMPL=see BASE=3
      'Betu$_x$ said Yermo$_y$ saw him.$_{x,*y,*z}$'   (MP 63)

Based on evidence from reflexives and dependent clauses, then, we can say that the above generalization is true between a main clause and a dependent clause as well. That is, the overt form can only co-refer with another overt form and a zero form can co-refer with either a full NP or a zero form, but not an overt form.

4.1.3 Adverbial clauses

Similarly, the overt form in a pre-posed adverbial clause cannot refer cataphorically to an NP in the main clause (14):

(14) ŏra   guéedábé$_1$ lá, ze   Bĕtu$_2$ nisa   quĕ
      o^{LH}ra gu^{LH}=eeda^{LH}=be^{LH} la^H z.e' Be^{LH}tu nisa   que^{LH}
      when POT=come=3.HUM   LA FUT.drink Betu   water DIST
      'When he$_{*x,y}$ comes, Betu$_x$ will drink that water.'   (MP 10)

Here, the use of the overt form in the adverbial clause does not co-refer with the subject NP of the main clause. Instead, a zero form must be used (15):

(15) ŏrá   guéedá$_1$ lá, ze   Bĕtu$_1$ nisa   quĕ
      ŏra   gu=eeda^{LH}=∅ la^H z.e'   Be^{LH}tu nisa   que^{LH}
      when POT=come=3   LA FUT.drink Betu   water DIST
      'When he$_{x,*y}$ comes, Betu$_x$ will drink that water.'   (MP 10)

To be clear, between an adverbial clause and a main clause, the overt form will co-refer with another overt form and a zero form will co-refer with either a full NP or a zero form.

Having observed the various syntactic environments conditioning the use and co-reference of both the overt and the zero form, the following sections explore the choices that speakers make in assigning one or other of these pronouns to referents in discourse.

4.2 The overt versus zero alternation in a Pear Story monologue

In the following excerpt from a re-telling of the Pear Story, the speaker initially assigns the overt third person form to the man picking pears, line 04, and the zero form to the boy on the bicycle, line 08. However, in line 14, the overt form is now used to refer to the bike boy, in the moment he rides past a new participant, the bike girl (for clarity, the overt form is marked using [1] and the zero form using [2]):

(16) 01 bihuiini   lu ni   lá,
            bi=huiini   lu ni^{LH} la^{H}
            COMPL=appear face 3SG.INAN LA

            'There appears,'

     02 ti rígola cuchuugu   caadxi cuánanaxhi
            ti ri^{H}gola c.u=chuugu' caadxi^{LH} cuananaxhi
            one man   PROG.CAUS=cut few   fruit

            'a man cutting some fruit.'

     03 rígola que lá,
            ri^{H}gola que^{LH} la^{H}
            man   DEM   LA

            'That man,'

     04 má   bichabe[1]   chúpá dxúmí ní
            ma'^{H} b.i=cha=be^{LH} chupa^{LH} dxumi^{LH} ni
            already COMPL.CAUS=fill=3.HUM two   basket   REL

            bíchuugubě[1]
            bi=chuugu=be^{LH}
            COMPL=cut=3.HUM

            'he had already filled two baskets of pears that he cut.'

     05 raque cúchabe[1]   guíra pěra
            raque^{LH} c.u=cha=be^{LH} guira^{LH} pe^{LH}ra
            then   PROG.CAUS=put.in=3.HUM all   pear

cuchuguběₐ

cu-chugu=beᴸᴴ

PROG=cut=3.HUM

'Then he was putting in all the pears he was cutting.'

06 dxí'babe₁   lú   yaga quě
    dxi'ᴴba=beᴸᴴ lu   yaga queᴸᴴ
    climb=3.HUM face tree DIST

    '(He was) up in that tree.'

07 qué   ñannadíbé₁   bédanda   tí
    queᴴ ña-nnaᴸᴴ-di=beᴸᴴ   be-dandaᴸᴴ   ti
    NEG   IRR=know-EMPH=3.HUM COMPL=arrive.there one
    xcuídihuiini
    xcuiᴴdi-huiini
    boy-DIM

    'He didn't know a boy arrived there.'

08 dxí'ba₂   ti   bicicléta
    dxi'ᴴba=∅   ti   bicicleᴴta
    PART.climb=3 one bicycle

    '(He was) on a bicycle.'

09 gucaa₂   ti   dxumi pěra   quě
    gu=caa=∅   ti   dxumiᴸᴴ peᴸᴴra queᴸᴴ
    COMPL=put=3 one basket   pear   DIST

    '(He) put that basket of pears.'

10 bidxí'ba₂   lu   xpicicléta₂
    bi=dxi'ᴴba=∅   lu   x=bicicleᴴta=∅
    COMPL-climb=3SG face POSS=bicycle=3

    '(He) got on his bicycle.'

11 ne   bíree₂   ze₂
    neᴸᴴ bi=ree=∅   z.e=∅
    and   COMPL=leave=3 PART.go=3

    'And (he) left.'

12 gula'na   xcuídi que   dxúmí pěra   stiě₁
    gu=la'na   xcuiᴴdi queᴸᴴ dxumiᴸᴴ peᴸᴴra stiᴸᴴ=beᴸᴴ
    COMPL=steal boy   DEM basket pear   POSS=3.HUM

    'That boy stole his basket of pears.'

13 huaxa neza ze   xcuídi   que   lá,
    huaxa neza z.e   xcui^{H}di que^{LH} la^H
    but   path PART.go boy   DEM   LA

    'But on the path as the boy was leaving,'

14 málasi   bídxagabe$_1$ tí   badudxaapahuiini
    ma^{H}lasi^{LH} bi=dxaga=be^{LH} ti   badudxaapa-huiini
    suddenly   COMPL=cross=3.HUM one girl-DIM

    'Suddenly he crossed a little girl'

15 dxí'ba$_2$ sti   bicicléta
    dxi'^{H}ba=∅   sti   bicicle^{H}ta
    PART.climb=3 other bicycle

    '(She was) on another bicycle.'   (*Pear Stories* TVA: 4–18)[2]

Before line 14, the narrator refers to the bike boy using the zero form. After line 14, the bike boy is referred to using the overt form. This switch in third person form announces or prepares the hearer for the introduction of the girl, who is thereafter referred to using the zero form. The bike boy, the most highly thematic participant, is referred to using the overt form for most of the remainder of the narration up until the very end, when focal attention is again paid to the pear man, who is then referred to using the overt form.

This alternating use of the overt and zero third person forms to refer to different characters in the Pear Story is consistent across the Pear Story corpus. The pear man is consistently assigned the overt form. The bike boy is initially assigned the zero form when he is introduced as a participant, is then assigned the overt form when the bike girl appears, and is then assigned the zero form again when the pear man returns to the scene. The bike girl and the boy with the paddleball are consistently referred to using the zero form. The use of the overt and zero forms across the Pear Story narratives can be summarized schematically this way:

Again, this pattern is consistent across all of the Pear Story narratives in the corpus. The overt form is never used with either the bike girl or the boy with the paddleball. Conversely, the zero form is never used with the pear man. The use of the overt form coincides with the more thematic participant at each particular juncture in the narrative. This is surprising given the strong cross-linguistic tendency for highly topical participants to be zero-coded, and for overt coding to signal a change of topic or indicate a less topical participant. In the Pear Story

---

[2]See Appendix A.

Table 4.1: Third person forms assigned to Pear Story referents

	Overt form	Zero form
Pear man	✓	
Bike boy	✓	✓
Bike girl		✓
Boy with paddleball		✓

narratives, therefore, ZAI speakers use the distinction between the overt and zero third person forms to assign referents varying degrees of thematicity. In the next section, I illustrate a similar use in conversation.

4.3 The overt versus zero form in conversation

In a similar way to the use in narratives described above, the overt-zero alternation can be used productively in dialogue not only to distinguish between two third-person participants but also to mutually construe one as more or less thematic than the other. The following example is taken from a conversation between two men, VA and CH. VA is asking CH about his father and goes on to ask how long each of CH's parents lived. Note, in particular, the intervention in line 06 by VA, where a zero third person form is assigned to CH's mother (again, for clarity, the overt form is marked using [1] and the zero form using [2]):

(17) (VA and CH, 27 Sept 2012)

01 VA: panda   íza bibani   bixhozelu'?
        panda^{LH} iza bi=bani   bixhoze=lu'
        how.many year COMPL=live father=2SG

        'How many years did your father live?'

02 CH: nabanibe$_1$ cérca de ochénta
        na=bani=be^{LH} ce^{H}rca de oche^{H}nta
        STAT=live=3SG.HUM close   to eighty

        'He lived close to eighty.'

03 VA: xheelabe$_1$ yá'?
        xheela'=be^{LH} ya'
        spouse=3SG.HUM Q

        'And his wife?'

04 CH: xheelabe$_1$ lá,
xheela'=be^{LH} la^H
spouse=3SG.HUM LA

'His wife,'

05 CH: laaca gúdi'dibe$_1$ séténta también
laaca^{LH} gu=di'di'=be^{LH} sete^{H}nta tambien^H
also   COMPL-pass=3SG.HUM seventy also

'she also passed seventy.'

06 VA: ah, laa$_2$ nírú   gúti$_2$
ah laa=∅ ni^{LH}ru^{LH} gu=ti=∅
INTJ BASE=3 front   COMPL=die=3

'Ah, (she) died first.'

07 CH: priměru   laaběͅ$_1$
prime^{LH}ru laa=be^{LH}
first   BASE=3SG.HUM

'First him.'

08 VA: ah laabe$_1$ má'   gutiběͅ$_1$
ah laa=be^{LH} ma'^{H} gu=ti=be^{LH}
INTJ BASE=3SG.HUM already COMPL=die=3SG.HUM

'Ah, he already died.'

09 CH: priměru   laaběͅ$_1$
prime^{LH}ru laa=be^{LH}
first   BASE=3SG.HUM

'First him.'

10 VA: ah laabe$_1$ jmáca huaniisibe$_1$ qué jñaalu'   ya'?
ah laa=be^{LH} jma^{H}ca huaniisi=be^{LH} que^H jñaa=lu' ya'
INTJ BASE=3SG.HUM more   old=3SG.HUM M   mother=2SG Q

'Ah, he was older than your mother?'

11 CH: laabe$_1$ jmá huaniisiběͅ$_1$
laa=be^{LH} jma^H huaniisi=be^{LH}
BASE=3SG.HUM more old=3SG.HUM

'He was older.'

12 CH: udi'dibe$_1$ lú binnigŏla qué zuluá'   bia'
gu=di'di'=be^{LH} lu binnigo^{LH}la que^{LH} z.ului'=a'^{H} bia'
COMPL=pass=3SG.HUM face oldperson DEM   FUT.seem=1SG like

          tapa iza
          tapa iza
          four year

          'He passed the old person, I think, by about four years.'

13 CH: peru udi'dibe$_1$ zuluá'   bia' tapa iza lu
          peru gu=di'di'=be^{LH} z.ului'=a'^{H} bia' tapa iza lu
          but COMPL=pass=3SG.HUM FUT.seem=1SG like four year face

          jñaa'
          jñaa=a'^{H}
          mother=1SG

          'But he passed my mother by four years.'

14 CH: jmá huaniisibe$_1$ xcáadxi
          jma^H huaniisi=be^{LH} xcaadxi
          more old=3SG.HUM some

          'He was a bit older.'

15 VA: ¿dxiiña ra ñaa guzaabe$_1$ dé
          dxiiña ra ñaa gu-zaa=be^{LH} de
          work   LOC field COMPL-complete=3SG.HUM from

          nahuiinibe$_1$ lá?
          na-huiini=be^{LH} la^H
          STAT-small=3SG.HUM Q

          'Did he work in the fields since he was little?'

In line 5, CH states that his father's wife, i.e. his mother, passed away when she was seventy. He refers to her using the overt form. In the next line, line 6, VA intervenes to ask whether his mother had passed away before his father, but refers to her using the zero form. In line 7, CH corrects VA and responds by saying *primeru laabe* 'first him', using the overt form to make clear that it was his father who passed away first, not his mother. In line 8, VA picks up on the use of the overt form and uses it again to check that he has understood correctly, saying *ah laabe ma gutibe* 'ah, he already died'. In line 9, VA confirms this, repeating *primeru laabe* 'first him', using again the overt form to refer to his father. The use of the overt form to refer to the father continues throughout the rest of the interaction.

One of the outcomes of VA's turn in line 6, then, is that the zero form is assigned to refer to CH's mother and the overt form is assigned to refer to his father. Rather than using a full NP to disambiguate reference, VA relies on the contrast between the two third person forms to create a contrast between the father and mother. It is not a coincidence that the overt form was chosen to refer to the father, as he is the more thematic figure and the center of this conversational episode. In contrast, the zero form is used for the mother, the less thematic figure.

This contrast between the overt enclitic and the zero form in third person is similar to the proximate/obviative contrast in Algonquian languages, in which proximate forms are used for the third person most central to the discourse and the obviative forms for more peripheral third persons (Dahlstrom 1991; 2003; 2014).[3] As with the proximate/obviative opposition, it would be interesting in future work to explore the extent to which the overt/zero alternation in ZAI can be sensitive to other factors such as empathy, agency, and point of view.

4.4 Summary and conclusions

This chapter summarized the pragmatic status of the two types of third person pronominal forms, the zero and the overt subject enclitic form, and explored the distribution and alternation of these forms in narrative and conversation. In addition to showing the syntactic facts governing the distribution of the overt and zero forms, this section showed that an important factor governing their use is the relative thematic salience of the referents, wherein the overt pronoun is used for more thematic figures and the zero for less thematic figures. Again, the ZAI data is unusual in this regard as one would expect the reverse: highly topical participants to be zero-coded and less topical participants to be coded with overt forms.

Chapter 6 takes the analysis made in this chapter as a basis to consider the relationship between cognitive status and topichood and the expression of topic relations between discourse referents and propositions. As will be seen, while cognitive status is not a prerequisite for topichood, topic referents usually have a certain degree of pragmatic accessibility such that more acceptable topics are higher on a cognitive status scale. First, I turn to an analysis of focus structure in ZAI, which is the subject of the next chapter.

---

[3]See, in particular, Dahlstrom (2014) in which the author argues that the definitions of both proximate or obviative cannot be reduced to that of topic or focus.

5 Focus structures in ZAI

In this chapter, I move away from the discussion of the specific forms of ZAI nominals and the ways that these signal more or less accessible referents and turn towards an analysis of the information structure categories of topic and focus. Topic and focus relations involve the relations not between discourse referents and accessibility but between discourse referents and propositions. That is, in similar sentences uttered in different contexts, the cognitive status of two referents may be the same, but the function – i.e. topic or focus – may be different; as such, cognitive status is only a precondition for the expression of these functions (Lambrecht 1994). The analysis below focuses on pragmatic phenomena that have particular correlates in clause or sentence structure. As we will see from the analysis that follows, the flexible nature of constituent order in ZAI is an important resource for ZAI speakers in organizing information structure.

This chapter aims to show that ZAI is a verb-initial language that displays flexible syntax whose linear order is strongly motivated by the pragmatic function of the utterance. In particular, linear order is determined in large part by decisions made by the speaker with respect to what the proposition is about, what is contextually dependent, what is pragmatically presupposed, and what is asserted. Chapter 6 explores related phenomena from the perspective of ZAI topic relations.

In this chapter, I investigate the organization of focus structure in ZAI again with an emphasis on the ways that the various typological characteristics of the language – phonological, morphological, and syntactic – interact with each other. The ZAI data supports the hypothesis that ZAI speakers mark focus relations primarily through the manipulation of constituent order and/or through morphological marking (for other Zapotec languages, see Broadwell 1999; Lee 2000) rather than through prosodic means. There does not seem to be any evidence for any pitch accents directly associated with focal material, although elements may display various prosodic properties – duration, pitch register, and pitch range – that may be related to the position within a given intonation unit in which they appear.

The chapter begins with a discussion of focus structure in ZAI and an analysis of the conceptualization of Lambrecht (1994) as it applies it to the ZAI data. In the section that follows, I introduce the typology of focus structure proposed by Van Valin (1999) and examine the place of ZAI within that typology. I then present and discuss a conversational strategy by ZAI speakers involving the parallel, chiastic use of predicate focus and argument focus to accomplish specific conversational goals.

5.1 Focus structure

The term *focus structure* (Lambrecht 1994) refers to the grammatical means by which a language indicates the scope of the assertion in an utterance and differentiates it from the presupposed or topical material.

The main contrast in focus structure is between broad focus and argument focus. Whereas in broad focus the focus domain extends over more than one constituent, in argument focus the focus domain extends only over one constituent. In broad focus constructions –which invariably involve verb-initial structures in ZAI– the verb is part of the assertion. In narrow focus constructions, the verb is part of the presupposition. In ZAI, narrow focus constructions tend strongly to not be verb-initial. The relevant generalization is the following: the verb will form part of the focus domain unless the construction is an argument focus construction, in which case it forms part of the presupposition.

There are two types of broad focus, predicate focus and sentence focus. I address these in turn.

5.1.1 Predicate focus

Predicate focus is traditionally referred to as a topic-comment construction, in which the subject is the topic and the predicate is a comment on that topic.[1] This is the unmarked focus type. The following examples from Lambrecht (1994) illustrate this focus construction type in four different languages: English, Italian, French, and Japanese. The sentences represent a prototypical response in each respective language to the question "How's your car?" which establishes "my car" as the topic (boldface indicates focal stress).

(1) Q: *How's your car?*
  a. *My car/it broke **down**.* English
  b. *(La mia macchina) si è **rotta**.* Italian
  c. *(Ma voiture) elle est en **panne**.* French
  d. *(Kuruma wa) **koshoo**shita.* Japanese

---

[1]Predicate focus is discussed in §6.1.2 in terms of topic-comment constructions.

In each case, the predicate is a comment or assertion about the subject-topic "my car". In English and Italian, the subject NP is the topic. In French, it is a detached NP, and, in Japanese, it is a *wa*-marked NP. In each of these languages the order of constituents is S-V and there is focal stress on the verb.

The realization of predicate focus is substantially different in ZAI, where predicate focus constructions are verb-initial:

(2) guxhiiñe   xcoché'
    gu-xhiiñe'   x=coche=e'[H]
    COMPL-break.down POSS-car=1SG

    'My car broke down.'

Although the subject-topic may be a full NP, as above, a subject pronominal clitic is more common:

(3) guxhiiñeni̱
    gu-xhiiñe'=ni[LH]
    COMPL-break.down=3.INAN

    'It broke down.'

The predicate thus occupies the clause-initial position in ZAI followed by the subject-topic, which can be realized as an enclitic or as a full NP.[2]

Below is a second example of a prototypical predicate focus construction in ZAI:

(4) Q: What did the boy do?
    bidxaagabe   tí   dxaapahuiini'
    bi-dxaaga=be[LH]   ti   dxaapa-huiini'
    COMPL-encounter=3.HUM one girl-DIM

    'He encountered a girl.'

This is a transitive clause where the subject-topic, 'the boy', appears as an enclitic on the verb and the predicate, 'encountered a girl' is the comment or assertion about the subject-topic. Again, this is a verb-initial construction.

The verb and the object are in the focus domain in this case, but neither receives focal stress in the form of a pitch accent. There is a gradual downdrift in pitch from the beginning of the clause to the end, but no specific pitch accent

---

[2] Predicate focus with a transitive verb and two full NP arguments would require the topical subject NP to appear before the verb. However, because topical subjects are very rarely coded using full NPs, this word order occurs in my corpus only in elicitation contexts.

occurs on either the verb or the object. The one H tone in the clause surfaces on *ti* as a result of the floating tone from the third person enclitic *=be*. This can be observed in the pitch track of this utterance shown in Figure 5.1 below:

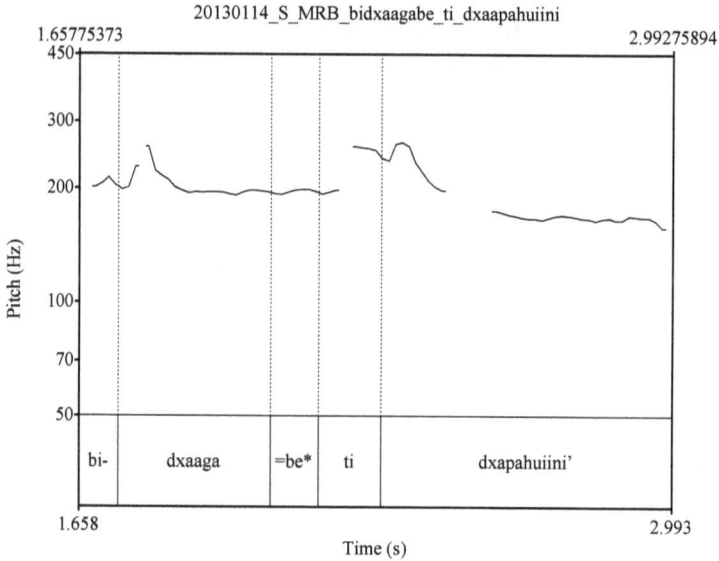

Figure 5.1: Pitch track

In general, elements that appear at the beginning of the intonation unit are pronounced with longer duration, a higher pitch register and wider pitch range, i.e. properties associated with beginnings and endings of intonation units. In this case, it is the verbal constituent that occurs in the prosodically more prominent position, the beginning of the intonation unit. The object NP constituent occurs in the next most prosodically prominent position, the end of the intonation unit.

Consider, now, the following example, taken from conversation:

(5) (M 18 March 2012, 08:47.0-08:52.0)

01 bibané lá,
   bi-bani=a$^{'H}$ la^H
   COMPL-wake.up=1SG LA
   'I woke up,'

02 guzé xa
   gu-zi=a$^{'H}$ xa
   COMPL-shower=1SG INTJ
   'I showered,'

90

03 güé   ti jŭgo de narănjasi   xá
    gü-e-a'^{H} ti ju^{LH}go de nara^{LH}nja-si^{LH} xa
    COMPL-drink=1SG one juice of orange-only   INTJ

'I drank an orange juice only.'

Here, the speaker remembers and tells about the sequential events during a morning routine. Each of the three lines is a predicate focus construction. Each clause
is verb-initial, with the narrator as the subject-topic and each predicate advanc-
ing the events in the narrative.

As seen in Figure 5.2, in this case as well, there is no pitch accent associated
with any of the constituents of the sentence.

20120318_C_TVA_02_gue_ti_jugo

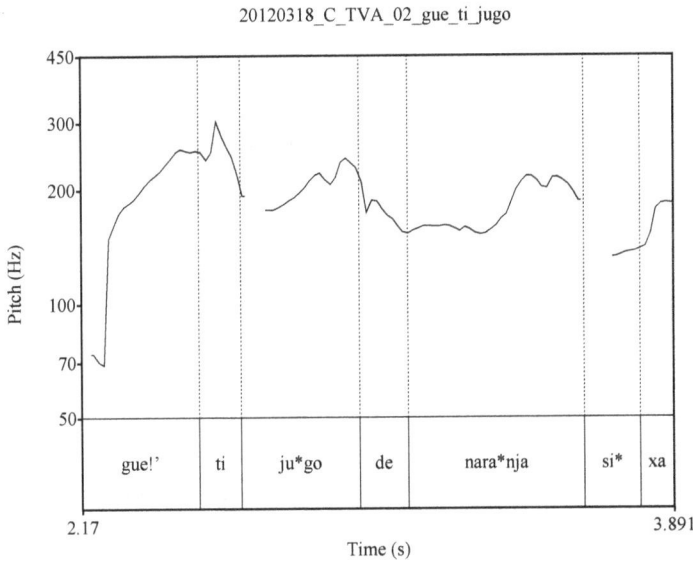

Figure 5.2: Pitch track

In the last line, line 3, The H and LH tones that surface can be directly attributed
to the underlying tones. The verb *güe* carries an H tone from the first person
enclitic. The NPs *jugo* and *narănja* both carry an LH tone on the stressed syllable,
as is characteristic of many Spanish loanwords. Finally, the particle -*si* attached
to the object NP contains a floating H tone that surfaces on the final particle *xa*.

The principal characteristic of predicate focus constructions in ZAI, therefore,
is that they involve a verb-initial main clause. Again, the verb is part of the focus
domain and does not receive focal stress in the form of a pitch accent. Additionally, there is a gradual downdrift in pitch from the beginning of the clause to the

end, but no specific pitch accent occurs on the object either. Below, we will compare predicate focus constructions to argument focus constructions in which a different constituent may occupy the pre-verbal position. First, I discuss sentence focus constructions, which are also verb-initial.

5.1.2 Sentence focus

I turn now to sentence focus.[3] In these, there is no topical subject and the focus domain is the entire sentence (again, examples are from Lambrecht 1994).

(6) Q: What happened?

a.	*My **car** broke down.*	*English*
b.	*Mi si è rotta la **macchina**.*	*Italian*
	Lit. 'Broke down to me the car'	
c.	*J'ai ma **voiture** qui est en panne.*	*French*
	Lit. 'I have my car which broke down'	
d.	***Kuruma** ga koshooshita.*	*Japanese*

Unlike the examples of predicate focus listed in (1), each of the sentences in (6) lacks a presupposed topic and, instead, the entire sentence is asserted. English uses the same syntactic construction as in (1); however, in this case the subject NP receives focal stress. In Italian, the focal stress still falls on the final constituent of the sentence, but the syntactic construction is altered so that the focused subject NP appears sentence-finally. In French, both the focal stress and the syntactic construction differ from (1) and a part of the information is now communicated via a relative clause. In Japanese, both the subject and the verb receive focal stress and the subject is marked using the morpheme *ga* rather than *wa*.

In ZAI, the construction is formally identical to the predicate focus construction in (2), except in this case there is no option to represent the subject as an enclitic. It must appear as a lexical NP:

(7) guxhiiñe   xcoché'
     gu-xhiiñe'   x=coche=e'[H]
     COMPL-break.down POSS-car=1SG

     'My car broke down.'

---

[3]Sentence focus is discussed again in §6.1.1 in terms of presentational or event-reporting constructions.

As we will see in the discussion of event-reporting constructions in §6.1.1, the most common use of sentence focus constructions is presentational constructions, to introduce new participants to a discourse. Consider the following example taken from a Pear Story narrative:

(8) bihuinni   ti rígola
     bi-huinni   ti ri^Hgola
     COMPL-appear one man

     'A man appeared.'

In a typical use such as this, the narrator uses a sentence focus construction to introduce a participant into the discourse. As with predicate focus, this is also a verb-initial construction which places the verb in the most prominent prosodic position. The intransitive subject is introduced as an indefinite noun and occupies the position at the end of the intonation unit. There is no topical subject and the focus domain is the entire sentence. Here, again, there is no special pitch accent associated with this construction.

5.1.3 Argument focus

While predicate focus and sentence focus are both types of broad focus, argument focus involves narrow focus. In argument focus, the focus domain is a single constituent, which may be an object, subject, adjunct, or even a verb (examples are from Lambrecht 1994).[4]

(9) Q: I heard your motorcycle broke down.

a.	My **car** broke down.	English
a'.	It's my **car** that broke down.	
b.	Si è rotta la mia **macchina**.	Italian
	Lit. 'Broke down my car'	
b'.	È la mia **macchina** che si è rotta.	
	Lit. 'It's my car that broke down'	
c.	C'est ma **voiture** qui est en panne.	French
	Lit. 'It's my car that broke down'	
d.	**Kuruma** ga koshooshita.	Japanese

---

[4]Argument focus is discussed in §6.1.3 in terms of identificational constructions.

In these sentences, the focus domain is restricted to the NP *car*. The presupposition is that 'something broke down' and the assertion is that it was the speaker's car and not something else that broke down. English again uses the same syntactic S-V-O construction and, as in (6), the subject NP again receives focal stress. In Italian, the syntactic construction is altered in such a way that the focal stress again falls on the final constituent of the sentence. In French, both the focal stress and the syntactic construction again differ from (1) and (6), with a part of the information again being communicated via a relative clause. In Japanese, the subject is marked using the morpheme *ga* (as in (6d)), and only the subject NP receives focal stress.

In argument focus it is possible for the focused NP to occur post-verbally in ZAI, but this is much less common and the preferred order is the following, where the focused NP constituent appears pre-verbally in clause-initial position:

(10) xcoché'   guxhiiñe'
      x=coche=e'^{H} gu-xhiiñe'
      POSS-car=1SG COMPL-break.down

      'My CAR broke down.'

Below is an example taken from conversation:

(11) (T and M, 18 March 2012, 16:03.0-16:06.0)

      01 T: ¿tu lá   bini   ganár, este, primér lugár?
             tu^{LH} la^{LH} b-ini   ganar^H este primer^H lugar^H
             who name COMPL-do win   INTJ first   place

             'Who won, um, first place?'

      02 M: ti   militár bini   ganár dxiquĕ
             ti   militar^H bi-ini   ganar^H dxique^{LH}
             one soldier COMPL-do win   then

             'A SOLDIER won then.'

Here, the question in line 1 by speaker V introduces the presupposition 'x won first place'. Speaker M responds in line 2 with the assertion 'x is a soldier' and uses a construction in which the subject appears in pre-verbal position followed by the verb which forms part of the presupposition. The most prominent prosodic position is occupied in this case by the subject NP.

Consider the following example, also of an argument focus construction. Here, the speaker's own statement in line 1 sets up a presupposition which is followed in line 2 by an argument focus construction.

(12)   (M, 18 March 2012, 10:20.5-10:23.5)

   01   nin   quí ñahuadiá   de endaré   gastí'

       nin   qui ñ-ahua-di=a$^{\text{'H}}$ de guendaro=a$^{\text{'H}}$ gasti$^{\text{'H}}$

       not.even NEG IRR-eat/drink-NEG=1SG of food=1SG   nothing

       'I didn't even eat/drink any of my food.'

   02   jŭgo   quesí   gué'

       ju^{LH}go que^{LH}-si^{LH} gu-e=a$^{\text{'H}}$

       juice   DEM-only   COMPL-eat/drink=1SG

       'I drank ONLY THE JUICE.'

Note first that the verb 'to eat/drink' is the same verb in line 1 as in line 2, the phonological form of the verb is conditioned by the TAM prefix. In line 1, the speaker sets up the presupposition 'I ate/drank x'. He continues in line 2 with the assertion 'x is only the juice.'

It is not the verb but an NP constituent that is in the prosodically prominent position at the beginning of the intonation unit. As above, however, there is no particular pitch accent associated with any particular part of the utterance (Figure 5.3).

20120318_C_TVA_02_jugo_que_si_gue

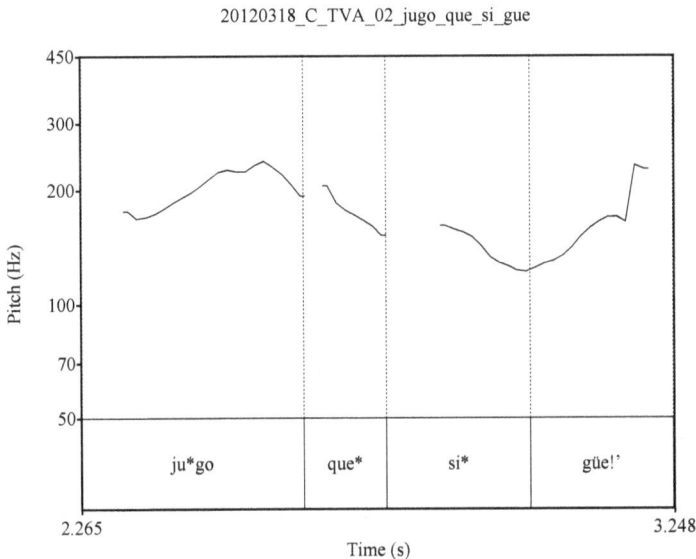

Figure 5.3: Pitch track

We can compare this construction to the predicate focus construction, '*gue ti jugo de naranjasi xa*' in (5) uttered by the same speaker. The constructions carry almost identical propositional content, except that in (5) the speaker uses an indefinite object NP and in (12) uses a definite object NP. The two utterances differ also in the order of constituents, with the object NP occurring pre-verbally in the argument focus construction (5) and post-verbally in the predicate focus construction (12). I return to pairs of utterances such as these in §5.2, where I discuss the patterned use of predicate focus followed by argument focus in conversation and explore the combined discourse function of the two constructions.

First, it should be noted, however, that argument focus constructions do not have to be NP-initial. A construction such as the following, with a verb-initial structure, would also be acceptable in the same situation:

(13) gué   jŭgo   quesĭ
      gu-e=a'^{H} ju^{LH}go que^{LH}-si^{LH}
      COMPL-eat/drink=1SG juice   DEM-only

      'I drank ONLY THE JUICE.'

There is no formal marking that separates this construction from a predicate focus construction, leaving it formally ambiguous. However, an NP in pre-verbal position unambiguously signals the focal nature of the NP. In verb-initial constructions, focus may fall on the verb. Only contextual information allows the participants to understand that the presupposition and assertion in the verb-initial version remain the same as in the original construction of line 2 in (12). Still, while a verb-initial structure can alternatively be used to communicate argument focus, the use of a pre-verbal constituent will always signal argument focus, unless the pre-verbal element is a subject NP and a resumptive pronominal clitic appears on the verb, as in the case of topicalization (see §6.1.4).

In the following section, I turn to a related argument focus construction involving the use of the particle NGA.

5.1.4 The use of NGA in argument focus

The particle NGA carries an H tone and is used in two types of constructions. One is in copulative constructions, such as in (14), where NGA, according to Pickett et al. (1998: 94), "emphasizes" the subject:

(14) laabe   ngá máistru
      laa=be^{LH} nga^H mai^{H}stru
      base=3SG NGA teacher

      'HE is a teacher.'   (Pickett et al. 1998: 94)

In this example, the independent pronoun functions as the subject of the clause, followed by NGA, and then *maistru* 'teacher'. This construction contrasts with the alternative copulative construction involving a zero-copula:

(15) máistru laabě
      mai^{H}stru laa=be^{LH}
      teacher base=3SG

      'He is a teacher.'

These two constructions differ in that while (14) is a type of argument focus construction, (15) is an example of predicate focus.

The NGA particle may be used in other constructions as well. It may be used to "emphasize" a subject of a transitive clause, as in (16):

(16) naa ngá bi'né   ni̯
      naa nga^H bi-i'ni=a' ni^{LH}
      1SG NGA COMPL-d=1SG 3INAN

      'I am the one who did it.'   (Pickett et al. 1998: 98)

In these cases, a co-referring dependent pronoun appears as an enclitic on the verb. In addition, it may be used to "emphasize" a direct object, as in (17).

(17) Juán nga biiyalu   neegue'
      Juan^H nga^H bi-uuya=lu' neegue'
      Juan NGA COMPL-see=2SG yesterday

      'It was Juan who you saw yesterday.'   (Pickett et al. 1998: 98)

The function of the NGA particle to provide "emphasis", as described by Pickett et al. (1998), can be understood in terms of Lambrecht (1994) as narrow or argument focus. Yet, it differs from argument focus constructions in which NGA is not present. Example (17) is not identical to (18), the corresponding argument focus construction without the particle NGA:

(18) Juán biiyalu   neegue'
      Juan^H bi-uuya=lu' neegue'
      Juan COMPL-see=2SG yesterday

      'You saw JUAN yesterday.'

The sentence in (17) requires an exhaustive listing interpretation where it was Juan and only Juan who the hearer saw yesterday. Meanwhile, the corresponding sentence without NGA in (18) requires only an information focus interpretation in which the hearer saw Juan yesterday but may have seen others as well.

An example from a Pear Story narrative illustrates the use of NGA further. Here, NGA appears in the third line after the phrase *suerte stibe* 'his luck'.

(19)   01   ne   biába   tambiěn   dxumí   quě
             ne^{LH} bi-aba   tambien^{LH} dxumi^H que^{LH}
             and   COMPL-fall   also   basket   DIST

             'And the basket fell also.'

       02   ne   lǎabé   támbiěn
             ne^{LH} laa=be^{LH} tambien^{LH}
             and   BASE=3SG   also

             'And he (fell) also.'

       03   suěrte   stibé   ngá   gaxha nuu   cádxi xcuídi   casi
             suer^{LH}te sti^{LH}=be^{LH} nga^H gaxha n-uu^{LH} cadxi xcui^{H}di casi
             luck   POSS=3SG   NGA   close STAT-be   some child   almost
             laabě
             laa=be^{LH}
             BASE=3SG

             'It was lucky for him there were some kids close to him.'   (*Pear Stories*, V: l.15–17)

The narrator is describing an event in the Pear Story in which the boy as well as the basket of pears he is carrying fall from the bike. The narrator uses a construction involving the particle NGA in the third line to accomplish two important discursive goals. First, the narrator introduces a new participant into the discourse, a group of three boys walking by (who would eventually help him). Second, the narrator points out that, contrary to the listener's expectations, the boy was fortunate to have fallen where he did right as the boys were there. The use of NGA after the first constituent, *suerte stibe*, not only marks the end of the assertion that the boy was lucky, it also separates this constituent from the rest of the utterance which introduces the boys.

Finally, in this last example, taken from a conversation between J and T, T responds to a question by J about whey and explains that one of the uses of the whey is as feed for pigs. T concludes his turn with an argument focus construction using NGA in line 5:

(20) (T 26 May 2012 (05:15.0-05:20.0))

    01 J: ¿xi   rúnicabe   né   suĕru?
             xi^{LH} runicabe^{LH} ne^{LH} sue^{LH}ru

             what HAB-do=PL-3.HUM with whey

             'What do they (people) do with whey?'

    02 T: laani   lá,
             laani^{LH} la^{H}

             BASE=3.INAN LA

             'As for it (the whey),'

    03 T: nabé rusirooni   bíhui
             nabe^{H} ru-si-roo=ni^{LH} bihui

             very HAB-CAUS-big=3.INAN pig

             'It really makes the pigs grow.'

    04 T: ngue   rúni
             ngue^{LH} ru-ni

             DEM   HAB-do

             'That's why,'

    05 T: stale   bínní   ngá   riquiiñenĭ
             stale^{LH} binni^{LH} nga^{H} ri-quiiñe=ni^{LH}

             much person NGA HAB-use=3.INAN

             'MANY PEOPLE use it.'

In this example, J asks T a question in line 1. T begins his response in line 2 using a LA-marked phrase to establish the whey as the topic referent for the next clause. In lines 3–5, T explains that, because feeding pigs whey causes them to grow, many people use it. His use of the particle NGA in the last line marks the statement as an argument focus construction with the subject NP *stale binni* 'many people' as the focused constituent. Because it is a focused constituent, there is no resumptive subject enclitic on the verb.

    It is interesting to note that in this example it is the object NP, the whey, that appears as an enclitic on the verb, not the subject. We would expect the pronominal object to appear as an independent form, not a dependent form, yielding the following utterance with the same propositional content: *stale binni nga riquiiñe laani*. The use of the third person enclitic forms for inanimate objects, as in line 5, is actually not an uncommon use and one that requires more attention in future work. I have heard it myself on many occasions in informal settings, but have not yet encountered it in my corpus, so I have little to say about it at this point. One hypothesis is that it is perhaps the role of the object NP as object-topic in this construction that allows it to appear as such and that this is a change in progress.

In summary, in this chapter we have observed the following pattern in the information structure of ZAI: while sentence focus and predicate focus constructions are consistently verb-initial, argument focus constructions contain either pre-verbal constituents (within the clause) or may be verb-initial. That is, constituent order in ZAI adapts to discourse functions. Pre-verbal elements are exclusively part of the focus domain, whether argument focus or sentence focus.

There is no evidence for any pitch accents directly associated with either topical or focal material, although elements may display various prosodic properties– longer duration, higher pitch register, and greater pitch range– that may be related to the position within a given intonation unit in which they appear. Focused elements (either nominal or verbal constituents) tend to occur in prosodically more prominent positions, i.e. beginnings of intonation units. The elements that appear at the beginning of intonation units are pronounced with longer duration, a higher pitch register and wider pitch range, i.e. properties associated with beginnings of intonation units.

From this perspective, given the range of functions available in the verb-initial position, ZAI appears to classify as relatively rigid pragmatically since the domain of focus appears to be confined to the pre-verbal position, but as syntactically relatively flexible since the verb-subject-object order is not always strictly adhered to. I turn to this discussion in the next section.

5.1.5 Van Valin's (1999) typology of focus structure

It is clear from the preceding discussion that languages can differ greatly in focus structures and in the linguistic resources they have for carrying out various discourse functions. One of the dimensions in which languages can differ is the syntactic dimension, whereby languages can be more or less rigid in terms of the syntactic arrangement of constituents. As the examples above show, a language such as English, for example, appears to have a more rigid syntax than languages such as French or Italian. Another dimension is that of the focal domain, including the placement of focal stress, whereby languages can be more or less rigid in terms of where the focal domain may lie within a given clause. This observation is the basis for a typology of focus structure proposed by Van Valin (1999), which I review here.

Lambrecht (1994) conceptualizes focus structure and focus types across languages using the notions predicate focus, sentence focus, and argument focus that were reviewed and discussed in the previous section. Based on Lambrecht's conceptualization, Van Valin (1999) proposes a way of comparing and classifying languages in terms of the relative degree of rigidity or flexibility in their constituent order and the relative degree of rigidity or flexibility in their focus structure. The distinction between rigid and flexible constituent order was discussed above in §2.3. While English is a language that fairly rigidly conforms to an S-V-O order, we have seen that the constituents of a ZAI clause are relatively flexible.

Central to his analysis of focus structure as relatively rigid or flexible is Van Valin's use of the notion "potential focus domain." Van Valin (1999: 513) defines "potential focus domain" as "the part of the sentence in which a focal element may potentially be found." In English, for example, the potential focus domain is the entire main clause, meaning that focal stress can potentially fall on any constituent within the main clause, such as the predicate or the right edge of a clause (see (1a)), or on a pre-verbal subject (see (6a), (9a)). English is an example of a language with relatively flexible potential focus domain.

The classification of languages in the two dimensions of rigid or flexible, on the one hand, and syntax and focus structure, on the other, yields a framework from which to view language diversity, for which Van Valin offers the following two-by-two typology: This way of classifying languages is based on whether the order

Table 5.1: A typology of focus structure (Van Valin 1999)

	Rigid focus structure	Flexible focus structure
Rigid syntax	French	English
Flexible syntax	Italian	Russian

of constituents in main clauses is primarily dependent on syntactic principles (e.g. grammatical relations) or on pragmatic ones (e.g. the (assumed) cognitive status of referents involved). On the one hand, constituent order may be constrained by pragmatic principles. For instance, a language may forbid the assignment of focus to pre-verbal subjects, as in Italian, or reserve a specific syntactic position for particularly "newsworthy" information, as in Cayuga (Mithun 1992). That is, the domain of focus assignment may be more or less fixed (typically with respect to the verb). On the other hand, in those languages where constituent order is more tightly constrained by syntactic principles, such as English, the encoding of information structure is frequently carried out exclusively by prosodic means, leaving constituent order intact.

Given that the distinction between rigid and flexible is meant to be understood as a continuum rather than as a binary distinction, based on the data reviewed so far, we can determine where the potential focus domain of ZAI falls on the continuum from rigidity to flexibility and, more generally, where ZAI focus structure may be located within Van Valin's typology.

In terms of focus structure, the potential focus domain in ZAI is relatively flexible, given that focused constituents can appear either pre-verbally or post-verbally. While in broad focus constructions (i.e. sentence or predicate focus), the focus domain is post-verbal, in narrow focus constructions there is a strong preference for focused constituents to appear pre-verbally, though post-verbal focused constituents are possible. Lexical NPs, whether pre- or post-verbal, are usually part of the focus domain, as are pre-verbal independent pronouns. Pre-verbal lexical NPs may be either focused NPs or topicalized NPs. In contrast, pronominal enclitics are always topical.

In terms of syntax, ZAI is also relatively flexible as arguments as well as non-arguments may occur pre- or post-verbally, oftentimes dictated by the needs of focus structure. It appears, therefore, that focus structure is more rigid than syntax, since focus structure may motivate certain syntactic arrangements while the reverse rarely, if ever, holds. That is, syntactic structure does not appear to motivate changes in the focus domain. In this way, ZAI may tend more towards the Italian-type rather than the Russian-type. This can be represented schematically as follows:

Table 5.2: ZAI in Van Valin's (1999) typology of focus structure

	Rigid focus structure	⟺		Flexible focus structure
Rigid syntax	French	⟹ ?	⟺	English
↕	↕			↕
Flexible syntax	Italian	⟺	ZAI ⟺	Russian

Although focus marking in ZAI does not involve pitch accent, focused material may appear only at the beginning or end of an intonation unit, i.e. positions of prosodic prominence. One possible motivation, therefore, for the range of constituent orders observed in the various ZAI construction types, as well as the distinction between broad and narrow focus types, may indeed be prosodic. In verb-initial structures, where the verb appears in the prosodically most prominent position, the verb strongly tends to form part of the assertion. In non-verb-initial structures, where non-verbal elements occupy the prosodically most prominent position, the verb forms part of the presupposition. In other words, if the verb is the initial element in the clause, it forms part of the focus domain. Otherwise, as in typical cases of argument focus, a non-verbal constituent in the pre-verbal clause-initial and prosodically most prominent position signals its focal nature.[5]

5.2 Focus structures in discourse: predicate focus plus argument focus

Above, I have reviewed the various types of focus constructions available to ZAI speakers. We have seen a number of ways in which speakers exploit various combinations of nominal forms and constituent orders to achieve their discursive goals with respect to the communication of topic and focus relations within a clause or sentence. In the final section of this chapter, I wish to expand this perspective by analyzing three related examples in which the specific combination of predicate focus followed by argument focus is employed in spontaneous discourse for specific ends. We will see that as well as expressing topic and focus relations, the combined use of these construction types aids speakers in accomplishing specific, additional interactional goals.

In the following example, the speaker is recounting what he ate the night before an important event in his life. He explains how he was hungry that night and ate as he normally would:

(21) (M, 18 March 2012, 8:31.0-8:37.0)

    01 má   candaaná   gueela'
         ma'^{H} ca-ndaana=a'^{H} gueela'
         already PROG-be.hungry=1SG night

         'I started to be hungry at night.'

    02 udahuá   normál
         gu-dahua'^{H} norma^{H}l
         COMPL-eat.1SG normal

         'I ate normal (as I normally would).'

---

[5] As will be seen in §6.1.4, subject NPs in topicalization constructions also appear in the initial, most prominent position in the clause. Similarly, in §6.2 we will see that LA-marked phrases, with their topic announcing or topic promotion function, are set off in a separate intonation unit altogether, among other things offering the phrase prosodic prominence.

03 normál   udahuá'
    norma^H l gu-dahua'^H
    normal   COMPL-eat.1SG

    'I ate NORMAL (as I normally would).'

The speaker mentions he was hungry that night in line 1 and follows this in line 2 with a topic-comment or predicate focus construction in which he states that he ate as he normally would, *udahua normal*. Interestingly, he follows this in line 3 with an argument focus construction, *normal udahua*, the mirror image of the utterance in line 2. In terms of a pragmatic assertion, however, there is little that line 3 adds to the hearer's understanding of the event. The information that the speaker ate as he normally would that night has already been transmitted.

There is no additional pitch accent associated with any part of either utterance, as we can observe in the pitch track shown below. We can also see, however, that there is no substantial pause between line 2 and line 3. In fact, line 3 is begun at the pitch level that line 2 ends with (Figure 5.4).

20120318_C_TVA_02_udahua_normal

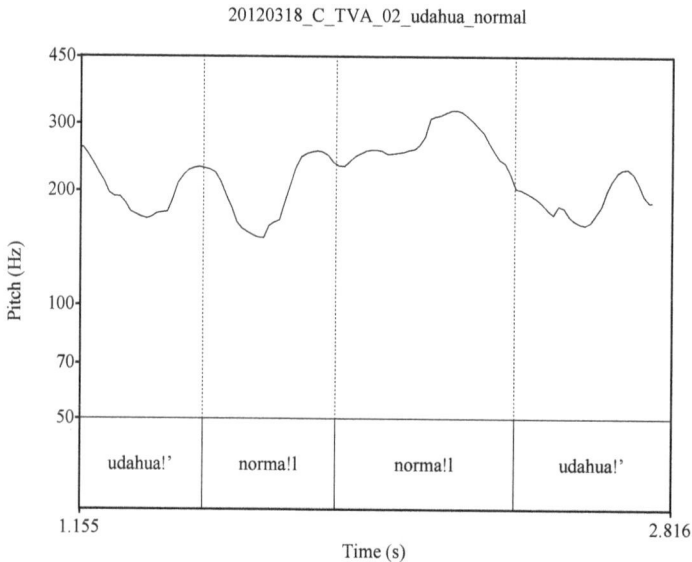

Figure 5.4: Pitch track

The use of the predicate focus construction followed immediately by argument focus may be conceptualized as a discursive structure of its own which exploits the "parallelism" (Jakobson 1966; Fox 1977) of the mirror image syntactic structures employed.[6] One of the functions of this parallelism, or "chiastic structure" (Silverstein 1984), is to help the speaker extend his speaking turn for an additional intonation unit. At the same time, the predicate focus plus argument focus combination together mark the end of the speaker's turn. The speaker cedes the floor, though not before providing a captivating end to the re-telling of a seemingly routine and uneventful night of eating. More importantly, the use of the chiastic structure binds the two intonation units into a couplet to be interpreted together.

This combined use of predicate focus plus argument focus as a chiastic structure is employed often in conversation between ZAI speakers. Below is a second example. Here, the speaker is talking about his participation in an international marathon in Mexico City 25 years prior and uses the chiastic structure of predicate focus plus argument focus in lines 2–3 to highlight his young age at the time:

(22) (T and M, 19 March 2012, 0:58.0-1:04.0)

01 T: dxi   bixooñé   jaa maratón internacionál qué   lá,
       dxi   bi-xooñe=a$^{'H}$ jaa marató!n internacional^H que^{LH} la^H
       when COMPL-run=1SG INTJ marathon international   DEM   LA

       'When I ran the international marathon,'

02 T: má   napá   veintidós iza
       ma$^{'H}$ n-apa=a$^{'H}$ veintidos^H iza
       already HAB-have=1SG twenty-two year

       'I was twenty-two years old.'

03 T: veintidós iza   napá   dxiquě
       veintidos^H iza   n-apa=a$^{'H}$ dxique^{LH}
       twenty-two year HAB-have=1SG then

       'I was TWENTY-TWO then.'

After beginning his turn with a LA-marked adverbial phrase in line 1 which introduces the event of the international marathon as topical, the speaker uses a predicate focus construction in line 2 to remark on his age at the time. In line 3, the speaker repeats the semantically equivalent utterance, this time using an argument focus construction in which his age appears pre-verbally.

In the final example, also from conversation, a similar use of the parallel, chiastic structure is used. This time the particle NGA can be observed. In the first two lines, T asks C what kinds of crops his father used to grow on his plot of land and whether he had cattle. C responds in lines 3–8.

---

[6]I thank Richard Rhodes for useful comments on this point.

(23) (T and C, 27 Sept 2012, 1:33.5-1:49.0)

01 T: ¿xi   bídxí'babe   yá'?
       xi^{LH} bi-dxi'^{H}ba=be^{LH} ya'
       what COMPL-grow=3.HUM Q
       'What did he grow?'

02 T: ¿gupabe   yŭzé   lá?
       gu-apa=be^{LH} yu^{LH}ze^{LH} la^H
       COMPL-have=3.HUM cattle   Q
       'Did he have cattle?'

03 C: bidxí'babe   pŭru   xubá'
       bi-dxi'^{H}ba=be^{LH} pu^{LH}ru xuba'^{H}
       COMPL-grow=3.HUM only   maize
       'He only grew maize.'

04 C: purtí   cheri   lá,
       purti^H cheri^{LH} la^H
       because here   LA
       'Because around here,'

05 C: pŭru   ngă   ngá rudxí'bacabĕ
       pu^{LH}ru nga^{LH} nga^H ru-dxi'^{H}ba=ca=be
       only   DEM   NGA HAB-grow=PL=3.HUM
       'Only that is what they grow.'

06 C: má   pŭru   xubá'
       ma'^{H} pu^{LH}ru xuba'^{H}
       already only   maize
       'Now just maize.'

07 C: ira   íxé   cámpesĭnu   nuu   lădú   rí   lá,
       guira'^{LH} ixe^{LH} campesi^{LH}nu n-uu^{LH} la^{LH}du ri'^{H} la^H
       all   all   peasant   STAT-be side   DEM LA
       'All the peasants here (lit. 'that are on this side'),'

08 C: má pŭru   xubá rudxí'bacabĕ
       ma'^{H} pu^{LH}ru xuba'^{H} r.u=dxi'^{H}ba=ca=be   LH
       now just   maize HAB=grow=PL=3.HUM
       'Now they grow only maize.'

In response to T's question in lines 1–2, C responds with a predicate focus construction in line 3, saying that his father only cultivated maize. In lines 4–5, he continues this thought stating that in that region maize is the only crop that was grown and does so using an argument focus construction involving the particle NGA. He repeats this thought again in line 6 in a verb-less clause. He ends his turn in lines 7-8 with an argument focus construction that is a mirror image of line 3.

Again, the use of the predicate focus construction followed immediately by argument focus can be conceptualized as a chiastic structure that exploits the parallelism of the mirror image syntactic structures employed. In using this parallel, chiastic structure, the two intonation units are bound into a couplet to be interpreted together, and the speaker extends his speaking turn for an additional intonation unit, with the second part, the argument focus construction, marking the end of the speaker's turn, thereby ceding the floor.

5.3 Summary and conclusions

In summary, this chapter explored the range of types of focus constructions in the ZAI data. As we saw, in the information structure of ZAI, sentence focus and predicate focus constructions are consistently verb-initial and argument focus constructions contain either pre-verbal constituents (within the clause) or, alternatively, may be verb-initial. A summary of these facts is shown in Table 5.3:

Table 5.3: Focus constructions in ZAI

Context	Example	Focus type	Constituent order
How's your car?	*guxhiiñenǐ*	Predicate focus	V-initial
What happened?	*guxhiiñe xcoché'*	Sentence focus	V-initial
I heard your motor-cycle broke down	*xcoché guxhiiñe'*	Argument focus	pre-verbal NP

In addition, this chapter showed that there is no evidence for pitch accents directly associated with focal material. However, elements may display various prosodic properties– longer duration, higher pitch register, and greater pitch range– related to their position within a given intonation unit. In particular, focused elements, be they nominal or verbal constituents, tend to occur in prosodically more prominent positions, i.e. beginnings of intonation units. Pre-verbal elements, for their part, are exclusively part of the focus domain. This was viewed as a possible prosodic motivation for the focus domain being associated primarily with the initial position, be it the verb in a verb-initial construction or a pre-verbal element.

These observations led us to examine the place of ZAI within the typology of focus structure proposed by Van Valin (1999). First, because arguments as well as non-arguments may occur pre- or post-verbally, we described ZAI as syntactically relatively flexible. Second, given that focused constituents can appear either pre-verbally or post-verbally, it was determined that the potential focus domain in ZAI is also relatively flexible. In broad focus constructions (i.e. sentence or predicate focus), the focus domain is post-verbal and, in narrow focus constructions, there is a strong preference for focused constituents to appear pre-verbally (though post-verbal focused constituents are possible). Lexical NPs, whether pre- or post-verbal, are usually part of the focus domain, as are pre-verbal independent pronouns.[7] In contrast, pronominal enclitics are always topical.

However, it does appear that focus structure is more rigid than syntax, since focus structure can motivate certain syntactic arrangements while the reverse never holds. That is, syntactic structure does not appear to motivate changes in the focus domain. Therefore, ZAI may tend more towards the Italian-type rather than the Russian-type (cf. Table 5.2).

Finally, the chapter concluded with a discussion of a conversational strategy used by ZAI speakers involving the successive use of predicate focus and argument focus to accomplish specific conversational goals. The use of the predicate focus construction followed immediately by argument focus was analyzed as a chiastic structure that exploits the parallelism of the mirror image syntactic structures employed. In using this chiastic structure, the two intonation units are bound into a couplet to be interpreted together, and the speaker extends his speaking turn for an additional intonation unit, with the second part, the argument focus construction, marking the end of the speaker's turn, ceding the floor.

---

[7]Pre-verbal lexical NPs may also represent topicalized NPs (cf. §6.1.4).

6 Topic relations in ZAI

The chapter discusses the linguistic resources available to ZAI speakers for expressing topic relations. This discussion of topic relations will set the stage for the analysis of a very commonly used topic-marking strategy involving the discourse particle LA.

In this discussion, I follow Lambrecht (1994) and use the term **topic** or **topic referent** to describe the referent or entity which the proposition is about. As such, the topic or topic referent is the referent or entity which bears a topic relation to the proposition. It is not to be confused with "old" information, which refers to the cognitive status of a referent. From this perspective, information which performs the role of topic in a given proposition may have a cognitive status that is either "old" or "new". On the givenness hierarchy discussed in §3.2, topic referents must be identifiable in the mind of the speaker and hearer, and continuous topics are usually also activated and familiar, but this is not a prerequisite for topic-hood. Instead, it is the relation that the topic referent or entity bears to the rest of the proposition that is significant. By contrast, the terms **topic constituent** or **topic NP** refer to the corresponding linguistic expression and not the referent or entity to which that expression refers.

Again, as was mentioned in the previous chapter, it is important to bear in mind that stress and pauses play a critical structural function in ZAI prosody (see §2.2). Pitch accents, however, do not play a role in the marking of topic or focus relations in ZAI.[1]

6.1 Topic constructions

In Chapter 3 we saw that the cognitive status of discourse referents has observable and direct correlates in ZAI grammar in terms of nominal forms and the grammatical roles – A, S, or O – in which they tend to occur. The cognitive status of referents correlates highly with the pragmatic acceptability of sentences

---

[1] We may keep in mind, as Crocco (2009: 15) states, that "the actual realization of the prosodic marking of topicality may vary according to the different positions occupied by the topic with respect to the prosodic nucleus of the utterance."

in other ways as well. For example, because insufficiently accessible topic referents are more difficult for hearers to interpret, topic referents tend to have a certain degree of pragmatic accessibility. Lambrecht (1994: 165) expresses this correlation in terms of a "Topic Acceptability Scale" by which more acceptable topics are coded by linguistic expressions that are higher on a cognitive status scale, such as the Givenness Hierarchy in Table 3.24, and less acceptable topics are coded by expressions which are lower on this scale. For ZAI, therefore, we would predict that the most acceptable topics would be coded by subject clitics, while the least acceptable topics would be coded by indefinite NPs or bare nouns.

In addition, we will see that there is also a correlation between the information structure of certain types of constructions and the cognitive status of the topic referents involved. In particular, in focus or activated referents do not occur in presentational or event-reporting constructions, and type-identifiable referents do not occur in "marked topic" or detachment constructions involving the particle LA. In other words, NPs in presentational constructions are never pronominal forms and NPs in detached, LA-marked constructions are never indefinite.

6.1.1 Presentational constructions

Cross-linguistically, statements about the weather tend to be thetic constructions.[2] An example is presented in (1):

(1) cayaba   nisaguie
     ca-yaba   nisa-guie
     PROG-fall water-stone
     'Rain falls.'

The construction is verb-initial and the lexical, subject NP is a bare noun. The subject is not topical and the focus domain is the entire sentence.

The following example from a Pear Story narrative shows an event-reporting construction with a presentational function:

(2) rihuinni   tí   rígola
     ri-huinni^{LH} ti   ri^{H}gola
     HAB-appear one man
     'A man appears.'

---

[2]Constructions such as these are also labeled "sentence focus"; see §5.1.2. They are sometimes also referred to as 'out-of-the-blue' sentences.

The construction, used to introduce a new participant into a discourse, is also verb-initial and here the subject is a lexical, indefinite NP. Again, there is no topical subject, the focus domain is the entire sentence, and it lacks a presupposed topic. In other words, it is thetic, i.e. the whole sentence is asserted.

In the Pear Story corpus, new referents are always introduced as lexical NPs, most often in the O role, followed by the S role, and much more rarely in the A role (see Table 3.8). When we take into account animacy, however, new referents are introduced at a higher rate in the S role than the O role (see Table 3.9). That is, the majority of human referents in the Pear Story corpus are introduced using presentational constructions of the type in (2). New referents introduced in the O role are introduced using topic-comment sentences, which I discuss in §6.1.2.

6.1.2 Topic-comment

In the following example from a Pear Story narrative, the subject in line 2 is the topic, and the predicate is a comment or assertion about the subject-topic.

(3) (*Pear Stories*, M: l.4)

    01   má   bihuinni   tí   señŏr
           ma'^{H} bi-huinni^{LH} ti   seño^{LH}r
           already COMPL-appear one man

           'A man appeared.'

    02   cuchuugube   pĕra
           cu-chuugu'=be^{LH} pe^{LH}ra
           PROG-cut=3SG   pear

           'He (was) cutting pears.'

The narrator uses a presentational clause in line 1 to introduce the man and, in the second line, uses a topic-comment construction to predicate a property (i.e. that he was cutting pears) about that man, an already established referent. The subject-topic in line 2 appears as an enclitic on the verb.

The subject NP, when topical, appears as an enclitic on the verb. In rare cases, such as in a transitive clause with a topical object, the subject NP may occur as a lexical NP. Invariably, however, like event-reporting constructions, topic-comment constructions in ZAI are always verb-initial (except in cases of topicalization or 'marked' topics). Therefore, because the verb-initial construction is compatible with other pragmatic construals, such as event-reporting or identificational constructions, we can consider the verb-initial topic-comment construction the unmarked type. I discuss identificational constructions next.

6.1.3 Identificational constructions

Also referred to as an argument focus construction (cf. §5.1.3), an identificational construction contains a topical argument and the focus domain is a single constituent. This focused constituent may occur in the O role, as in (4), a response to the question "What did he cut?":

(4) Q: What did he cut?
     pĕra   cuchuugube
     pe^{LH}ra cu-chuugu'=be^{LH}
     pear   PROG-cut=3SG
     'He was cutting PEARS.'

Here, the subject-topic in the A role appears as an enclitic on the verb and the focused NP in the O role is placed in pre-verbal position. It is just as acceptable and common, however, in the same communicative context, to respond with a verb-initial construction with the object in clause-final position, as in (5):

(5) (Q: What did he cut?)
     cuchuugube   pĕra
     cu-chuugu'=be^{LH} pe^{LH}ra
     PROG-cut=3SG   pear
     'He was cutting PEARS.'

Out of context, the construction in (5) is formally ambiguous between an identificational construction and a topic-comment construction. While the verb-initial construction can be interpreted as either, the object-initial construction can only be interpreted as an identificational construction.

In identificational constructions, the single focused constituent may also be an adjunct. As above, the adjunct may appear clause-initially (6) or clause-finally (7):

(6) (Q: How did he finish?)
     naguĕendá   bíluxebĕ
     na-guee^{LH}nda^{LH} bi-luxe=be^{LH}
     STAT-fast   COMPL-finish=3.HUM
     'He finished FAST.'

(7) (Q: How did he finish?)
     biluxebe   náguĕendă
     bi-luxe=be^{LH} na-guee^{LH}nda^{LH}
     COMPL-finish=3.HUM STAT-fast
     'He finished FAST.'

In (6), the focused constituent is an adverb and appears in pre-verbal position and the subject-topic again appears as an enclitic on the verb. In contrast, in (7), the subject-topic again appears as an enclitic on the verb but the focused constituent appears in clause-final position.

Finally, the single focused constituent in an identificational construction may also be a subject. Again, the focused subject can appear pre-verbally (8) or post-verbally (9):

(8)　Q: Who fell?
　　　badu que　　biába
　　　badu que^{LH} bi-aba
　　　boy　DIST　COMPL-fall
　　　'THE BOY fell.'

(9)　Q: Who fell?
　　　biaba　　　badu quĕ
　　　bi-aba　　　badu que^{LH}
　　　COMPL-fall boy　DIST
　　　'The boy fell.'

If, however, the subject is coded as a pronominal NP, it may only appear pre-verbally as an independent form, as in (10). Unlike dependent pronouns, independent pronouns are always stressed.

(10)　Q: Who fell?
　　　laabe　　　　biába
　　　laa=be^{LH}　　bi-aba
　　　BASE=3.HUM COMPL-fall
　　　'HE fell.'

The focused subject cannot appear as an enclitic, as shown in (11).

(11)　Q: Who fell?
　　　#biababĕ
　　　bi-aba=be^{LH}
　　　COMPL-fall=3.HUM
　　　'He fell.'

As an unaccented pronominal form, it is unsurprising that the subject enclitic cannot function as a focused constituent. This can be seen in transitive environments as well, where focused pronominal subjects in the A role must occur as independent pronouns in pre-verbal positions, as in (12):

(12)   Q: Who cut the pears?
      laabe   bíchuugu ca pěrá   quě
      laa=be^{LH} bi-chuugu' ca pe^{LH}ra que^{LH}
      base=3.HUM COMPL-cut PL pear   DIST
      'HE cut the pears.'

The semantically equivalent form with a pronominal subject enclitic is pragmatically inappropriate in the same context:

(13)   Q: Who cut the pears?
      ?bichuugube   ca pěrá   quě
      bi-chuugu'=be^{LH} ca pe^{LH}ra que^{LH}
      COMPL-cut=3.HUM PL pear   DIST
      'He cut the pears.'

In transitive constructions with a topical object, the focused subject constituent must appear before the verb, as in (14).

(14)   Q: Who cut the pears?
      rígola que   bíchuugu ca pěrá   quě
      ri^{H}gola que^{LH} bi-chuugu' ca pe^{LH}ra que^{LH}
      man   DIST   COMPL-cut PL pear   DIST
      'THE MAN cut the pears.'

Here, the object-topic appears as a bare NP in post-verbal position and the focused subject appears pre-verbally. If the subject appears as a lexical NP in the position immediately after the verb, the construction can only be interpreted as an event-reporting construction:

(15)   bichuugu rígola que   pěrá   quě
      bi-chuugu' ri^{H}gola que^{LH} pe^{LH}ra que^{LH}
      COMPL-cut man   DIST   pear   DIST
      'The man cut the pears.'

This construction would not be used as an answer to the question "Who cut the pears?". The only way for a lexical NP functioning as a focused subject in the A role to appear after the verb would be for the object NP to appear as an independent pronominal form, as in (16):

(16) Q: Who cut the pears?
bichuugu rígola que   laácáni
bi-chuugu' ri^{H}gola que^{LH} laa=ca=ni^{LH}
COMPL-cut man   DIST   BASE=PL=3

'THE MAN cut them.'

While acceptable, such a construction is not considered common or natural by the ZAI speakers with whom I worked and was produced only in elicitation settings.

In summary, based on the above discussion, two factors can be observed to interact closely in the expression of topic relations in ZAI: constituent order and nominal form. Verb-initial clauses are compatible with the widest range of pragmatic construals as they can be employed in event-reporting, topic-comment, and identificational constructions. Lexical NPs in any of these three construction types typically signal a constituent that forms part of the focus domain. Independent pronominal forms, for their part, may signal topical or focal material, depending on position and on context. Meanwhile, dependent forms, i.e. subject enclitics, are used exclusively for subject-topics. Pre-verbal constituents, whether subjects, objects, or adjuncts, are almost exclusively focused constituents of identificational constructions. One exception to this is the topicalization construction, which I turn to next.

6.1.4 Topicalization

Arguments that appear immediately before the verb form part of the focus domain (§6.1.3). This is the case in an identificational construction, where the focused constituent can be an object (4), an adjunct (6), or a subject (12). In a topicalization construction, however, a pre-verbal subject is followed by a resumptive subject enclitic on the verb, as in the following example:

(17) laabe   bíchuugube   pěra
laa=be^{LH} bi-chuugu'=be^{LH} pe^{LH}ra
base=3SG COMPL-cut=3SG   pear

'He cut pears.'

In contrast to (12) where the pre-verbal pronoun functions as a focused constituent, here the pronoun in pre-verbal position functions as a subject-topic, as signaled by the co-indexed subject clitic. The predicate is a comment on that topic.

Topicalization constructions typically occur with referents that have already been introduced. In the following example, the definite NP in pre-verbal position in line 4 refers to an already introduced referent (18):

(18)   (*Pear Stories*, T: l.25–27)

01   huaxa neza ze   xcuídi   que   lá,
     huaxa neza ze   xcui^{H}di que^{LH} la^H
     but   path PART.go boy   DIST   LA

'But on the path that the boy went la,'

02   málásí   bídxaagabé   tí   badudxaapahuiini
     ma^{H}lasi bi-dxaaga^{LH}=be^{LH} ti   badudxaapa-huiini
     suddenly COMPL-cross-3SG   INDEF girl-DIM

'Suddenly he encountered a little girl.'

03   dxí'ba   sti   bícícléta
     dxi'^{H}ba=∅   sti^{LH} bicicle^{H}ta
     PART.climb=3 other bicycle

'(She was) on another bicycle.'

04   badudxaapahuiini que   gúxha   ziña bandá   nuu
     badudxaapa-huiini que^{LH} gu-xha=∅   ziña banda'^{H} n-uu^{LH}
     girl-DIM   DIST   COMPL-knock=3 palm shade   STAT-be
     íquébě
     ique=be^{LH}
     head-3SG

'The little girl knocked off the hat that was on his head.'

A new participant in the discourse, the bike girl, is introduced in line 2 as an indefinite, lexical NP in the O role, *ti badudxaapahuiini* 'a little girl'. This referent appears again in pre-verbal position in line 4, as a definite NP in pre-verbal position, and coincides with a change in subject from the previous clause. This is not an identification construction, however, but a topicalization construction in which the bike girl is promoted to topic.[3]

There are two elements that permit the analysis of this construction as a topicalization construction rather than an identificational one. First, whereas in an identificational construction the predicate forms part of the presupposition, here

---

[3]There is, in fact, no difference in formal marking between the zero form and no subject enclitic. For this reason, the contrast between the two constructions can only be elicited in discursive contexts and then discussed with native speaker consultants who, in my experience, are then readily able to recognize the appropriate interpretation.

the predicate is a comment on the topic. There is nothing in the context that ties the predicate as already part of the discourse. Second, as we saw in the previous chapter, the zero third person pronominal enclitic form is commonly used by speakers to signal the bike girl as the less thematic participant. This is true in this particular narration of the Pear Story as well. In fact, the zero third person form was assigned to the bike girl in the previous intonation unit, in line 3. Line 4 is thus a topic-comment construction about the bike girl.

The following example further illustrates a similar topicalization construction, again from a Pear Story narrative:

(19) (*Pear Stories*, M: l.61–64)

01 iza'na   sombrĕru   que   rá   nŭubĕ
    gu-iza'na=∅   sombre^{LH}ru que^{LH} ra   n-uu^{LH}=be^{LH}
    COMPL-took=3SG hat   DIST   LOC STAT-be=3.HUM

'(He) took the hat to where he (the boy) was.'

02 laabe   bísiga'debe   láa   chonna   pĕra
    laa=be^{LH} bi-si-ga'de=be^{LH} laa=∅   chonna^{LH} pe^{LH}ra
    BASE=3.HUM COMPL-CAUS-give=3.HUM BASE=3SG three   pear

'He (the boy) gave him three pears.'

In line 1, the narrator uses a topic-comment construction to tell how one of the three boys, the boy with the paddleball, takes the hat to where the bike boy is. The boy with the paddleball functions as the subject-topic and is encoded using the zero third person enclitic. In line 2, the bike boy is promoted to topic through the topicalization construction. We see the use of the independent pronominal form in pre-verbal position which is followed by the resumptive subject enclitic. We also see the use of the zero third person form in this line to refer to the boy with the paddleball.

6.1.5 Detached or LA-marked constructions

One final sub-class of topic phrases is found with the particle LA where, similar to a topicalization construction, the NP appears before the verb and is co-indexed by a subject enclitic on the verb:

(20) laabe   lá,   cuchuugube   péra
      laa=be^{LH} la^{H} cu-chuugu'=be^{LH} pe^{LH}ra
      base=3SG DEM PROG-cut=3SG   pear

'As for him, he was cutting pears.'

Constructions such as that in (20) were addressed briefly above in §3.1.7.2. In contrast to the similar, semantically equivalent constructions in (12) and (17), here the NP is set off in a separate intonation unit marked by the particle LA and accompanied by an audible pause. In some contexts such here in (20), LA-marked phrases have a topic promoting function similar to a topicalization construction. In other contexts, however, LA-marked phrases can have additional discourse functions. What are the main functions of the LA construction, how does it compare cross-linguistically, and what are its uses in spontaneous conversation? This is the focus of the rest of this chapter.

6.2 Topic relations and the LA particle in discourse

The LA particle is used widely in ZAI discourse and does not have referential meaning, but interacts with constituent order and intonation. It carries a High tone and invariably appears at the end of an IU, followed by a pause (never anywhere else). In this section, I review the range of constructions in which LA occurs, including adverbial, conditional, and left-detached clauses, and assess its possible status as a topic marker. I conclude by exploring and commenting on the functions of LA in extended discourse and conversation.

LA is used consistently in temporal clauses that advance or give information about the sequence of events in a narrative, as in (21) and (22):

(21) (*Pear Stories*, T: l.28–29)

01 ŏra   bidxiguetalube   bíiyabe   bádudxaapa
    o^{LH}ra bi-dxiguetalu=be^{LH} bi-uuya=be^{LH} badudxaapa
    when COMPL-turn=3SG.ANIM COMPL-see=3SG.ANIM girl

    que   lá,
    que^{LH} la^{H}

    DIST   LA

    'WWhen he turned and saw that girl **la**,'

02 bidxelasaa   biciclétanebé   tí   guieroo'ba
    bi-dxela-saa   bicicle^{H}ta-ne^{LH}=be^{LH} ti   guie-roo'ba
    COMPL-find-RECIP bicycle-with=3SG.ANIM one stone-AUG

    'He crashed his bike against the rock.'

(22) (*Pear Stories*, Ts: l.8–9)

   01 raque   má   zeeda   tí   xcuídihuiini lá,
        raque^{LH} ma'^{H} zeeda^{LH} ti   xcui^{H}di-huiini la^{H}
        then   already PART.come INDEF boy-DIM   LA

        'Then as a little boy arrives **la**'

   02 biiyabe   rá   cuchuugu pěrá quě
        bi-iya=be^{LH} ra   cu-chuugu'=∅ pe^{LH}ra que^{LH}
        COMPL-see=3SG.ANIM when PROG-pick=3 pear   DIST

        'He saw he (the man) was cutting the pears.'

This use in temporal clauses is extremely common and, despite the fact that speakers do not deem it obligatory, it is rare to find cases in spontaneous speech in which LA is absent.[4]

    It is also possible to use LA discourse-initially:

(23) (*Lexu ne gueu*)

   01 Ni chigüeniá'   laatu   dí **lá**
        Ni chigüe-ne^{LH}=a'^{H} laa=tu^{LH} di'^{H} la^{H}
        REL POT.say-with=1SG base=3PL.ANIM DEM LA

        'This that I will tell you **la**'

   02 bizaacani   má   xadxi
        bi-zaaca=ni^{LH} ma'^{H} xadxi
        COMPL-happen=3SG.INAN already time

        'it happened some time ago.'

This discourse-initial use of LA has a similar function to the use of LA with temporal clauses mentioned above as it presents background knowledge or links elements of the discourse with the setting. The LA particle also appears consistently at the end of the initial phrase of conditionals, as in (24):

(24) Pa guiába   nisaguie   guixí   **la**, qué ziaá'
      pa^{LH} gui^{LH}-aba nisa-guie guixi'^{H} la^{H} que^{H} zi^{LH}-e=a'
      if   POT-fall   water-stone tomorrow LA NEG FUT-go=1SG

      'If it rains tomorrow **la**, I won't go.'   (Pickett et al. 1998: 109)

---

[4]A tentative hypothesis in this regard may be that this use could be related to the lack of temporal or tense information in the verb. ZAI verbs obligatorily take aspectual prefixes, although it is an open question to what extent those prefixes convey tense or mood information (cf. §2.3.1). More detailed study is required in this direction to determine whether this is the case.

Both adverbial and conditional clauses are known to be explicitly marked in other languages as well (see Thompson et al. 2007: 292). For example, in Hua (Papuan) topics, interrogatives, conditionals are marked with *ve* (Haiman 1978). In Turkish, a conditional suffix also marks topics (Kerslake 1996). Such adverbials and conditionals are not the only clauses to be marked as topics, as it is extremely common to find various types of adverbial clauses functioning as topics. Concession, reason, time and condition clauses in Chinese may all occur with the four topic/interrogative particles (Thompson et al. 2007: 293). In Godié (Kru (Ivory Coast)), a non-final morpheme occurs at the ends of adverbial clauses functioning as topics and single nouns which function as topics may also be similarly marked (Marchese 1977; 1987). In Lisu (Tibeto-Burman), adverbial clauses functioning as topics are marked with the same marker *nya* which is used for NP topics (Thompson et al. 2007: 294). In Karbi (Tibeto-Burman), the additive particle marks contrastive topics (Konnerth 2013). The same is true in Central Kurdish, where the additive particle marks topics as well as temporal, spatial clauses (Opengin 2013).

The question, therefore, is whether we can assume LA is a topic marker. According to Chafe (1976: 50) (see also Li & Thompson 1976), topics may have the following characteristics: a) they appear in sentence-initial position; b) they are discourse dependent; c) they need not be arguments of the main predication; d) they are definite; and e) they set a "spatial, temporal, or individual framework within which the main predication holds."

These facts fit with an analysis in which LA is involved in the marking of topical information. This does, in fact, appear to be the case, as LA can appear with topical NPs, but never with focused initial NPs:

(25) ¿tu   bí'ni'   nǐ?   Tomǎs   (*la) bi'ni   nǐ
      tu^LH bi-uni   ni^LH   Toma^LH s   bi-uni   ni^LH
      who COMPL-do 3SG.INAN Tomás   COMPL-do 3SG.INAN
      'Who did it? Tomás (*la) did it.'

There are several reasons why it is common for topical adverbial or conditional clauses to play this discourse cohesion role. First, background temporal or spatial clauses may function as a "scene-setting" topic for the matrix clause (Lambrecht 1994: 125). Second, their main function is to link the preceding clause with the clause to which they are attached and, at the same time, set a framework within which the following predication holds (Thompson et al. 2007: 294). Third, they serve to recapitulate already-mentioned material, i.e. to establish common ground between interlocutors. Finally, there is often a H pitch that appears on the end of the first intonation unit, then falling on the second. This helps bind the information into a couplet structure which allows for interpretation together (cf. §5.2; see also Sicoli (2007: 126–127).[5]

6.2.1 Left-detachment constructions

The topic-marking function of LA can be seen in left-detached constructions as well. In a left-detached construction, an active or accessible lexical or pronominal NP is set off from the matrix clause without a verb by the LA particle and a pause, and is then taken up again in the following matrix clause by a co-indexed element. In (26), line 3, taken from a Pear Story narrative, the narrator uses an independent pronoun followed by LA as well as by a pause in the intonation:

(26) (*Pear Stories*, Ts: l.30–33)

01 biabantaabĕ
    bi-abantaa=be^{LH}
    COMPL-fall.hard=3SG.ANIM

    'He fell.'

02 bireeche   dxumi   pĕra   stibĕ
    bi-reeche   dxumi^{LH} pe^{LH}ra sti^{LH}=be^{LH}
    COMPL-spill basket   pear   POSS-3SG.ANIM

    'His basket of pears spilled.'

03 **laabe**   **lá,**
    laa=be^{LH} la^{H}
    BASE=3SG.ANIM LA

    'He **la**,'

04 biiyadxisibe   bádudxaapahuiini quĕ
    bi-uuyadxisi=be^{LH} badudxaapa-huiini que^{LH}
    COMPL-look=3SG.ANIM girl-DIM   DIST

    'He looked at that little girl.'

The use of LA at the end of the intonation unit marks the referent of the independent pronoun, the bike boy, as the topic of the subsequent clause. This is also a different topic referent than the topic referent of line 2.

The signaling of a different main-clausal subject (or object), as well as a different topic, from the previous clause is an extremely common use of LA. Below is another example, this time from casual conversation:

---

[5]In this contrasting and textual cohesion function, the ZAI morpheme appears to have characteristics similar to the Somali morpheme *baa* reported in Matić & Wedgwood (2013: 138-140).

(27)   (*20070730_TVA*)

    01 xagueté nisa runidxi binnĭ
        xaguete^H nisa ru-nidxi binni^{LH}
        under   water HAB-dive person

        'Under the water people dive.'

    02 ne lú nisa lá,
        ne^{LH} lu nisa la^H
        and face water LA

        'And above water la,'

    03 rixuubacabĕ
        ri-xuuba'=ca-be^{LH}
        HAB-swim=PL-3SG.ANIM

        'they swim.'

After offering one alternative in line 1 to what people may do under the water, the speaker switches the topic in line 2, marked by the use of LA, to what people may do above water. In this way, the left-detachment construction marked by LA is often used to mark a shift in attention from one to another of two or more already topical referents.

To summarize briefly, we have observed thus far that the LA particle serves the following two main discourse functions: 1) it consistently appears at the end of sentence-initial adverbial clauses and conditionals, i.e. in a frame-setting or delimiting function, and 2) it may signal changes in topic or boundaries of topical units, i.e. as a contrastive topic marker. In this way, constructions with LA form part of the background presuppositions which, as Thompson et al. (2007: 292) note, "establish a framework within which to proceed with a discourse, in the same way a question does." In fact, all of the constructions involving LA that we have reviewed so far share a common morphology with yes/no questions.

6.2.2 Yes/no questions

Yes/no questions in ZAI are formed by the addition of a question marker that has the exact same form as a sentence-initial adverbial clause or conditional (also carries a H tone):

(28)   ¿riuuladxu'   Lulá lá?
      ri=yuu-ladxi=lu' Lula'^{H} la^H
      HAB=enter-gut=2SG Oaxaca LA

      'Do you like Oaxaca?'

There are three principal reasons to think this is the same morpheme as the discourse particle LA. First, as we saw in §2.3, it is uncommon in V-initial languages for question particles to occur in clause-final position (Payne 1990). Second, common morphology has been found cross-linguistically between interrogatives and conditionals (cf. Haiman 1978). Finally, conditional markers are known to consistently develop out of interrogative particles (König & Siemund 2007: 296).

A possible reason for the existence of such a connection in ZAI is that the LA particle is used by ZAI speakers as a resource in interaction for managing the common ground. More specifically, LA can be seen as a "try-marking" device (Sacks et al. 1974). Sacks et al. (1974) define a "try-marker" as the use of an accessible form, with upward intonation contour, followed by a short pause, possibly searching for confirmation of the referent from other participants (cf. Pekarek Doehler 2011). One way to think about this is to think of sentences that are marked with LA as similar to "mini-conversations" (Thompson et al. 2007: 292). For example, the conditional construction in (24) is semantically similar to (29):

(29)   A: *¿chi guiaba nisaguie guixí' la?* 'Is it going to rain tomorrow?'
       B: *ziaba* 'It will.'
       A: *que ziaá'* 'I won't go.'

Here, Speaker A uses a LA-marked phrase (similar to the protasis in the corresponding conditional construction in (24)) to seek confirmation from B in the form of a yes/no response. In this case, B's explicit response provides a shared ground within which A can proceed to effectively convey the main propositional content (the apodosis in the corresponding conditional construction), i.e. that he won't go.

The conditional construction, therefore, has a very similar interactional function, the main difference lying in the lack of an explicit response from an addressee after the protasis. It is an open question, however, to what extent ZAI speakers do or do not signal degrees of awareness of common ground through non-verbal means during conversation, as this varies cross-culturally. This is an important question to explore in future work.[6] In both cases, LA is used to mark the speaker's turn as a procedure for securing referential common ground with the addressee(s).

---

[6]From a usage-based perspective, this analysis suggests the notion of (action and grammatical) projection (cf. Auer 2005), in the sense that the use of a LA foreshadows a range of possible upcoming actions or constructions.

The use of LA with the function of securing referential common ground can also be seen in cases in which a speaker is constructing a list. An example is given in (30), taken from a casual conversation between three male adults. Here, LA is used in lines 2, 4, and 5.

(30) (*20120318_C_TVA*: 5:44-5:54)

    01 péru   ti   dxi ănte
          pe^{LH}ru ti dxi a^{LH}nte
          but   one day before

          'But one day before,'

    02 viĕrne   huaxhinni que **lá**
          vie^{LH}rne huaxhinni que^{LH} la^{H}
          Friday   evening   DEM   LA

          'that Friday evening **la**'

    03 uxudxidŭ
          gu=xudxi=du^{LH}
          COMPL=drink=1PL.EXCL

          'we got drunk.'

    04 laabe   **lá**
          laa=be^{LH} la^{H}
          base=3SG.ANIM LA

          'Him (pointing) **la**'

    05 Vidal **lá**
          Vidal la^{H}
          Vidal LA

          'Vidal **la**'

    06 ne   náa
          ne^{LH} naa
          and   1SG

          'and I.'

    07 bide'du   jmá cáguăma
          bi-de'=du^{LH} jma^{H} cagua^{LH}ma
          COMPL-drink=1PL.EXCL much beer

          'We drank lots of beer.'

The LA particle appears in line 2 at the end of an adverbial clause similar to the uses discussed above in (21) and (22). In line 4, the speaker uses the third person independent pronoun followed by LA to refer to one of his interlocutors (which he reiterates by simultaneously pointing). In the immediately following line, line 5, he refers to yet another third person referent (not a participant) using his first name followed by LA. He adds one final referent, himself, in line 6, without the use of LA. Those three individuals make up a group, established over three intonation units, who together function as the subject-topic in line 7 referred using the 1PL.EXCL enclitic. In this way, the LA particle is used by the speaker to help the addressee identify the individuals in question, i.e. secure common ground, prior to the predication (cf. Principle of the Separation of Reference and Role, Lambrecht 1994).

In addition to topic marking and topic promotion, then, the use of LA should be seen as a resource for organizing talk and for making that organization recognizable to the speech participants. This section has shown that an analysis of the multifunctional nature of LA depends on the analysis of spontaneous speech and, especially, of conversation. It may be useful to investigate the use of LA as a resource in the co-construction of talk, in floor-holding, in turn-taking, in turn entry points, etc. and, more generally, as a window into the ways in which listeners orient to speech and conversation. Because listeners in different speech communities may orient in different ways, the relevant question thus becomes: how might the use of the LA particle be tied to local conversational strategies and conversational norms? From this perspective, it is likely that a characterization of LA in terms of notions like topic and focus is insufficient, and that insight into its functions can be better understood through an analysis of talk-in-interaction, i.e. of the kinds of interactional work that are being done in conversation and how.

6.3 Summary and conclusions

This chapter has presented an analysis of the strategies available to ZAI speakers to mark various types of topics and topic relations. It explored the relationship between pragmatic or cognitive status and topic-hood and found that it is not a pre-requisite, but that topic referents usually have a certain degree of pragmatic accessibility, where more acceptable topics are higher on a cognitive status scale (i.e., the Topic Accessibility Scale, Lambrecht 1994). Because insufficiently accessible topic referents are more difficult to interpret, the most acceptable topics in ZAI were found to be clitics and the least acceptable to be indefinite NPs and bare nouns.

Two main factors, constituent order and nominal form, were observed to interact closely in the expression of topic relations in ZAI. Verb-initial clauses are compatible with the widest range of pragmatic construals as they can be employed in event-reporting, topic-comment, and identificational constructions. Lexical NPs in any of these three construction types typically signal a constituent that forms part of the focus domain. Independent pronominal forms, for their part, may signal topical or focal material, depending on position and on context. Meanwhile, dependent forms, i.e. subject enclitics, are used exclusively for subject-topics. Preverbal constituents, whether subjects, objects, or adjuncts, are almost exclusively focused constituents of identificational constructions. One exception to this is the topicalization construction. In TOPICALIZATION constructions, the pre-verbal constituent is a subject-topic with a co-referring enclitic on the verb. These are used typically in cases of topic promotion.

A correlation was identified between information structure and certain types of constructions and the cognitive status of the referents involved. For example, IN FOCUS (Gundel et al. 1993) or ACTIVATED referents do not occur in presentational or event-reporting constructions. Also, TYPE IDENTIFIABLE referents do not occur in "marked topic", detachment constructions involving the particle LA. Therefore, for ZAI, NPs in presentational constructions are never pronominal forms, and NPs in detached, LA-marked phrases are never indefinite.

It is important to note that the analysis of spontaneous speech and, specifically, of conversation makes possible a multifunctional analysis of LA. Through this analysis, we saw too that LA-marked constructions can have a topic-promoting function, but also mark topical information, set the spatial, temporal, or individual framework within which the predication holds, and play a discourse cohesion role. They mark phrases that function as "scene-setting topics" that have a frame-setting or delimiting function. LA-marked constructions also mark contrastive topics, indicating changes in topics or boundaries of topical units.

Furthermore, constructions with LA form part of the background presuppositions, and establish a framework within which to proceed with the discourse, in the same way a question does. LA is, in fact, used in yes/no questions to secure referential common ground with the addressee(s). As such, LA can be seen not only as a resource for marking various types of topical information, but more generally as a resource for organizing talk and interaction.

7 Conclusions and avenues for further research

The fundamental aim of information structure studies, and of discourse pragmatics more generally, is to understand how the same propositional content can be expressed in linguistically different ways. In this, it is important to examine the *syntagmatic* relations between the elements of a clause or sentence and the ways that these can vary. More crucially, however, the study of information structure requires an analysis of the *paradigmatic* relations between different, but related clause or sentence structures. These structures, as they are stored in the memory of speakers and hearers, represent alternative ways to structure propositions that differ depending on the pragmatic goals of the speaker. In other words, the study of information structure involves not only the relationships and orders between elements within a clause or sentence, but also the relationships between clauses or sentences that are semantically equivalent though formally and pragmatically different. These relationships are the paradigmatic relations that hold between available alternatives and that speakers and hearers bring to bear to accomplish their communicative goals.

This study examined the paradigmatic relations that hold in ZAI between different structures on two distinct levels: a) the pragmatic states of the referents of individual sentence constituents in the minds of the speech participants, and b) the pragmatic relations established between these referents and propositions. First, as we saw in Chapters 3 and 4, speakers use the relationships between nominal forms, cognitive statuses, and grammatical roles in nuanced ways to accomplish specific communicative and interactional goals, such as to 1) introduce and track referents, 2) mark referents as more or less accessible, and 3) mark certain referents as more or less thematic. Second, as we saw in Chapters 5 and 6, speakers exploit the relations between constituent orders, morphology, and topical and focal material to 1) distinguish between presuppositions and assertions, 2) mark shifts of background information or of topical units, 3) signal the focus domain of a proposition, and 4) to accomplish interactional goals such as holding or ceding the floor in turn-taking in conversation.

With these two directions in mind, this chapter presents an overview of the main contributions of this study. In this, I discuss the conclusions derived from the analysis of the main information structure properties of ZAI, namely: 1) nominal forms and cognitive status, 2) the LA particle, and 3) topic and focus constructions. This discussion includes the conclusions reached in the analysis of the use of each of these three properties in narrative and conversation including: the alternation between overt and zero third-person pronominal clitics, the use of the particle LA, and the parallel, chiastic use of predicate focus and argument focus. Included in each section is a discussion of possible avenues for further research.

7.1 Nominal forms and cognitive status

This study explored the relationship between form and distribution of nominals and between their form and function, analyzing the different forms that are used to introduce and track referents and to mark referents as more or less accessible. The discussion, framed between Preferred Argument Structure (Du Bois et al. 2003) and the theory of Accessibility (Ariel 2001), showed that the fundamental mechanism driving the tendencies captured by PAS can be traced to the notion of accessibility.

More specifically, the avoidance of new referents and lexical NPs in the A role was understood as an avoidance of referents in the A role with a low degree of accessibility. The tendency, in other words, is to *avoid low accessible As*. The result is that highly accessible referents with less coding material are likely to occur in the A role. In contrast, low accessible referents with more coding material are unlikely to occur in that role and, instead, will more consistently occur in the O role. The S role exhibits a tendency in between the A and O roles in that it will often house previously mentioned, animate, salient, topical, and recent referents. At the same time, however, it will often function as a "cognitive staging area" for the introduction of new referents at episode boundaries.

Moreover, because nominal forms indicate the status of their denotations as pragmatically more or less available in the speaker or hearer's mind, the forms of nominals that speakers use depend on the assumed cognitive status of the referents involved. That is, they depend on assumptions that a speaker can reasonably make regarding the addressee's knowledge and attention state in the specific context in which the form is used. Therefore, not only does type of nominal expression correlate with grammatical role, but with cognitive status as well.

It is important to note that pragmatic or cognitive status is not a pre-requisite for topic or focus-hood, although it may play a role. Because insufficiently accessible topic referents are more difficult to interpret, topic referents usually have a certain degree of pragmatic accessibility, where more acceptable topics are higher on a cognitive status scale (i.e., the Topic Accessibility Scale, Lambrecht 1994). The least acceptable are indefinite NPs and bare nouns. The most acceptable topics in ZAI are clitics. Related to this, it was observed that the inanimate object enclitic, although inconsistent, is employed relatively frequently for topics (cf. example (20)). One goal of future work should be to pay close attention to this use.

Correlations were also found between information structure of certain types of constructions and the cognitive status of the referents involved. IN FOCUS (Gundel et al. 1993) or ACTIVATED referents do not occur in presentational or event-reporting constructions. TYPE IDENTIFIABLE referents do not occur in "marked topic", detachment constructional involving the particle LA. Therefore, for ZAI, NPs in presentational constructions are never pronominal forms, and NPs in detached, LA-marked phrases are never indefinite. Presentational constructions are often used to introduce new, human referents, but new referents, either human or not human, can also be introduced in the O role using topic-comment constructions.

Chapter 4 focused on the pragmatic status of the two third person pronominal forms, the zero and the overt subject enclitic form, exploring the distribution and alternation of these forms in narrative and conversation. While the overt form was found to have a broader set of binding conditions than the zero form, the choice between the two forms is free at the main clause level. In those cases, an important discursive factor governing their use is the relative thematic salience of the referents. Because the overt pronoun is used for more thematic figures and the zero for less thematic figures, speakers must make active choices in contexts involving multiple third-person participants about which pronoun to assign to each. The study of narrative and conversational contexts is therefore crucial for understanding how speakers and hearers evaluate the relative thematicity of participants and use linguistic resources to do so.

7.2 Topic and focus constructions

At the center of information structure in ZAI is the flexible nature of constituent order. As we saw, the extent to which phonetic and intonational cues play a role in the expression of the cognitive status of referents was found to be minimal, and information structure categories and relations are expressed mainly through manipulation of constituent order.

Verb-initial clauses are compatible with the widest range of pragmatic construals as they can be employed in all topic-focus construction types: event-reporting, topic-comment, and identificational constructions. Constituent order, however, adapts to discourse functions, and verb-initial syntax in ZAI is frequently violated in constructions in which topicalized and focalized elements may often appear before the verb. For this reason, we described ZAI as syntactically relatively flexible. In addition, because the focus domain is mostly tied to the pre-verbal position, ZAI can be described as pragmatically relatively rigid. Pre-verbal constituents, whether subjects, objects, or adjuncts, are almost exclusively focused constituents of identificational constructions.[1]

Therefore, focus structure in ZAI may motivate certain syntactic arrangements. The reverse, that syntactic arrangements motivate changes in the focus domain, is never the case.

Moreover, constituent order interacts closely with nominal form in the expression of topic and focus relations in ZAI. Lexical NPs in any construction type typically signal a constituent that forms part of the focus domain. Independent pronominal forms, for their part, may signal topical or focal material, depending on position or context. Meanwhile, dependent forms, i.e. subject enclitics, are used exclusively for subject-topics. A focused subject cannot appear as an enclitic on the verb.

Finally, it was noted that both verb-initial and non-verb-initial structures exploit positions of prosodic prominence at the beginning and end of IUs. As we saw through an analysis of the use of different focus structure constructions in narrative and conversation, these positions are exploited in the parallel, chiastic use of predicate focus and argument focus.

In this sense, while there is no evidence for pitch accents associated with topical or focal material, it is possible that there may be a prosodic motivation for the various types of constituent orders and for the pragmatic motivations underlying their use. The search for description and explanation in this dimension would benefit greatly from a detailed, systematic study of the range of intonation patterns employed by ZAI speakers and their relation to the diversity of information structure categories and constructions. Ideally, this study could be extended or related to similar phenomena in related Zapotec languages.

---

[1]One exception to this is the topicalization construction, in which the pre-verbal constituent is a subject-topic with a co-referring enclitic on the verb. These are used typically in cases of topic promotion.

7.3 The LA discourse particle

The discourse particle LA is involved in expressing information structure in ZAI. As we saw in Chapter 6, LA-marked constructions can have a topic-promoting function, but also mark topical information, set the spatial, temporal, or individual framework within which the predication holds, and play a discourse cohesion role. They mark phrases that function as "scene-setting topics" can have a frame-setting or delimiting function, mark changes in topic or boundaries of topical units, and/or function as contrastive topic markers.

More generally, constructions with LA form part of the background presuppositions and establish a framework within which to proceed with the discourse, in much the same way that a question does. As was pointed out, there are, in fact, similarities between the use of LA in yes/no questions and in LA-marked or detached phrases in that both are used to secure referential common ground with the addressee(s). From this perspective, LA functions as a try-marker and as a resource for negotiating common ground.

As with the analysis of the overt versus zero alternation in third person pronominal forms, the multifunctional analysis of LA also requires the analysis of spontaneous speech and, specifically, of conversation. It is likely that the use of LA is tied to the ways that ZAI speakers signal degrees of awareness of common ground in interaction through not only linguistic means but also non-verbal means. An analysis of multi-modal interaction would no doubt be extremely worthwhile to begin to understand how forms such as this are employed and how they fit into local conversational norms about the kinds of assumptions that are made explicit linguistically between speakers and hearers and which are not.

Because listeners in different speech communities can orient themselves in different ways, the following question is posed: How can the use of the particle be linked to local conversational strategies and norms? From this perspective, probably a characterization of LA, as well as a more general characterization of the focal structure of the ZAI in terms of notions such as topic and focus is insufficient (see Matić & Wedgwood 2013; Ozerov 2015). Instead, it is likely that the uses of the focal structure will be better understood through an analysis of the interaction; that is, through an analysis of the types of interactions that participants are having in the conversation and why.

Appendix A

N: 01 ¿randa   guíní'lu   xi   biiyalu?
    r-anda^{LH} gui^{LH}-ni'=lu xi   bi-iya=lu
    2SG-be.able POT-say=2SG what COMPL-see=2SG

    'Can you tell what you saw?'

T: 02 zandá   pue
    z-anda^{LH}-a'^{H} pues^{H}
    FUT-can=1SG well

    'Well, I can'

N: 03 ¿xi   biiyalu?
    xi   bi-iya=lu
    what COMPL-see=2SG

    'What did you see?'

T: 04 bihuiini   lu   ni   lá
    bi=huiini   lu   ni^{LH} la^{H}
    COMPL=appear face 3SG.INAN LA

    'There appears,'

  05 ti   rígola cuchuugu   caadxi   cuánanaxhi
    ti   ri^{H}gola c.u=chuugu' caadxi^{LH} cuananaxhi
    one man   PROG.CAUS=cut few   fruit

    'a man cutting some fruit'

  06 rígola que   lá
    ri^{H}gola que^{LH} la^{H}
    man   DEM   LA

    'that man,'

07 má   bichabe   chúpá dxúmí ní bíchuugubě
    ma$^{\text{'H}}$ b.i=cha=be^{LH} chupa^{LH} dxumi^{LH} ni bi=chuugu=be^{LH}
    already COMPL.CAUS=fill=3.HUM two   basket REL COMPL-cut=3.HUM

    'he had already filled two baskets of pears that he cut'

08 raque   cúchabe   guíra pěra   cuchugubě
    raque^{LH} c.u=cha=be^{LH} guira^{LH} pe^{LH}ra cu-chugu=be^{LH}
    then   PROG.CAUS=put.in=3.HUM all   pear PROG=cut=3.HUM

    'then he was putting in all the pears he was cutting'

09 dxí'babe   lú   yaga quě
    dxi$^{\text{'H}}$ ba=be^{LH} lu yaga que^{LH}
    climb=3.HUM face   tree DIST

    '(he was) up in that tree'

10 qué ñannadíbé   bédanda   tí xcuídihuiini
    que^{H} ña-nna^{LH}-di=be^{LH} be-danda^{LH} ti xcui^{H}di-huiini
    NEG IRR=know-EMPH=3.HUM COMPL=arrive.there one boy-DIM

    'he didn't know a boy arrived there'

11 dxí'ba   ti bicicléta
    dxi$^{\text{'H}}$ba=∅   ti bicicle^{H}ta
    PART.climb=3 one bicycle

    '(he was) on a bicycle'

12 gucaa   ti dxumi pěra quě
    gu=caa=∅   ti dxumi^{LH} pe^{LH}ra que^{LH}
    COMPL=put=3 one basket   pear DIST

    '(he) put that basket of pears'

13 bidxí'ba   lu xpicicléta
    bi=dxi$^{\text{'H}}$ba=∅   lu x=bicicle^{H}ta=∅
    COMPL-climb=3SG face POSS=bicycle=3

    '(he) got on his bicycle'

14 ne   bíree   zě
   ne^{LH} bi=ree=∅   z.e^{LH}=∅
   and   COMPL=leave=3 PART.go=3

   'and (he) left'

15 gula'na   xcuídi   que   dxúmí   pěra   stibě
   gu=la'na   xcui^{H}di que^{LH} dxumi^{LH} pe^{LH}ra sti^{LH}=be^{LH}
   COMPL=steal boy   DEM   basket   pear   POSS=3.HUM

   'that boy stole his basket of pears'

16 huaxa neza ze   xcuídi   que   lá
   huaxa neza ze   xcui^{H}di que^{LH} la^H
   but   path PART.go boy   DIST   LA

   'but on the path that the boy went,'

17 málásí   bídxaagabé   tí   badudxaapahuiini
   ma^{H}lasi^{LH} bi-dxaaga^{LH}=be^{LH} ti   badudxaapa-huiini
   suddenly   COMPL-cross-3SG   INDEF girl-DIM

   'suddenly he crossed a little girl'

18 dxí'ba   sti   bícícléta
   dxi'^{H}ba=∅   sti^{LH} bicicle^{H}ta
   PART.climb=3 other bicycle

   '(she was) on another bicycle'

19 badudxaapahuiini que   gúxha   ziña bandá   nuu   íquébě
   badudxaapa-huiini que^{LH} gu-xha=∅   ziña banda'^{H} n-uu^{LH} ique=be^{LH}
   girl-DIM   DIST   COMPL-knock=3 palm shade   STAT-be head-3SG

   'the little girl knocked the hat that was on his head'

20 ǒra   bidxiguetalube   bíiyabe   bádudxaapa que
   o^{LH}ra bi-dxiguetalu=be^{LH} bi-uuya=be^{LH} badudxaapa que^{LHLH}
   when COMPL-turn=3SG.ANIM COMPL-see=3SG.ANIM girl   DIST
   lá
   la^H
   LA

   'when he turned and saw that girl'

21 bidxelasaa   biciclétanebé   tí   guieroo'ba
    bi-dxela-saa   bicicle^{H}ta-ne^{LH}=be^{LH} ti guie-roo'ba
    COMPL-find-RECIP bicycle-with=3SG.ANIM one stone-AUG

    'he crashed his bike against the rock'

22 biabantaabě
    bi-abantaa=be^{LH}
    COMPL-fall.hard=3SG.ANIM

    'he fell'

23 bireeche   dxumi   pěra   stibě
    bi-reeche   dxumi^{LH} pe^{LH}ra sti^{LH}=be^{LH}
    COMPL-spill basket   pear   POSS-3SG.ANIM

    'his basket of pears spilled.'

24 laabe   lá
    laa=be^{LH} la^H
    BASE=3SG.ANIM LA

    'he,'

25 biiyadxisibé   bádudxaapahuiini quě
    bi-uuyadxisi^{LH}=be^{LH} badudxaapa-huiini que^{LH}
    COMPL-see.fixedly=3SG.ANIM girl-DIM   DEM

    'he looked at that little girl.'

26 raque   lá
    raque^{LH} la^H
    LOC-DIST LA

    'then'

27 mála   ze   chonna   xcuídihuiini
    ma^{H}la   ze   chonna^{LH} xcuidi-huiini
    suddenly FUT.go three   kid-DIM

    'suddenly three little kids'

28 badunguiiuhuiini laacă
    badunguiiu-huiini laaca^{LH}
    boy-DIM   also

    'little boys also'

29 gucanecá   laabe   bídopa   guǐrá pĕrá quĕ
    gu-ca-ne^{LH}-ca=∅   laa=be^{LH} bi-dopa^{LH} guira^{LH} pe^{LH}ra que^{LH}
    COMPL-help-with-PL=3SG BASE=3SG COMPL-pick.up all   pear   DIST

    '(they) helped him pick up all the pears'

30 bichaacani   ní dxúmǐ
    bi-chaa=ca-ni^{LH} ni dxumi^{LH}
    COMPL-put.in=PL-3SG.INAM LOC basket

    'they were put in the basket'

31 ne   bídxi'babe   ní biciclétá stĭbĕ
    ne^{LH} bi-dxi'^{H}ba=be^{LH} ni bicicle^{H}ta sti^{LH}=be^{LH}
    and COMPL-climb=3SG LOC bicycle   POSS=3SG

    'and he got on his bicycle'

32 zizabĕ
    z-iza=be^{LH}
    PROG-walk=3SG

    'and went walking'

33 guiónna' badunguiuuhuiini que   lá,
    guio^{H}nna' badu-nguiiu-huiini que^{LH} la^{H}
    third   child-man-DIM   DIST LA

    'those three boys,'

34 gudí'dica,
    gu-di'^{H}di=ca-∅
    COMPL-cross=PL-3

    '(they) crossed,'

137

35 zěca
ze^{LH}=ca-∅
PROG.go=PL=3

'(they) were leaving'

36 ŏra   biiyaca   nexhe ziña bandá   stĭbé   lú   neza que
o^{LH}ra bi-iya=ca-∅   nexhe ziña banda'^{H} sti^{LH}=be^{LH} lu neza que^{LH}
when COMPL-see=PL-3 lying palm shade   POSS=3SG   face path DIST
lá
la^H
LA

'when they saw his hat lying on that path'

37 gundisácá   nĭ
gu-ndisa'^{H}=ca-∅ ni^{LH}
COMPL-lift=PL-3   3SG.INAM

'(they) picked it up'

38 ne   bíbiguetaca
ne^{LH} bi-bigueta=ca-∅
and COMPL-return=PL-3

'and went back'

39 bicaca   stiĭpí   laabě
bi-ca=ca-∅   stii^{LH}pi^{LH} laa=be^{LH}
COMPL-put=PL-3 whistle   BASE=3SG

'(they) whistled to him'

40 ne   gúyeca   ra   nuubě
ne^{LH} gu-ye=ca-∅   ra   n-uu=be^{LH}
and COMPL-go=PL-3 LOC STAT-be=3SG

'and (they) went to where he was,'

41 bidiica   ziña bandá' stĭbě
bi-dii=ca-∅   ziña banda'^{H} sti^{LH}=be^{LH}
COMPL-give=PL-3 palm shade   POSS=3SG

'(they) gave him his hat'

42 laabe ŏraque lá
   laa=be^{LH} o^{LH}raque^{LH} la^{H}
   BASE=3SG then   LA

   'then he,'

43 gucuabe chónná pĕra
   gu-cua=be^{LH} chonna^{LH} pe^{LH}ra
   COMPL-choose=3SG three   pear

   'he chose three pears'

44 bidiibe cá ba'du que né bíreĕbĕ
   bi-dii=be^{LH} ca ba'du que^{LH} ne^{LH} bi-ree=be^{LH}
   COMPL-give=3SG PL child DIST and COMPL-leave=3SG

   'he gave those kids and he left'

45 zinĕbé xpíciclétábĕ
   zi^{H}-ne^{LH}=be^{LH} x-bicicle^{H}ta=be^{LH}
   PROG.go-with=3SG POSS-bicycle=3SG

   'he went with his bicycle'

46 ca ba'du que lá
   ca ba'du que^{LH} la^{H}
   PL child DIST LA

   'those children LA'

47 gudi'dica neza
   gu-di'di=ca-∅ neza
   COMPL-pass=PL-3SG path

   '(they) crossed along the path'

48 zĕca
   ze^{H}=ca-∅
   PROG.go=PL-3

   '(they) left'

49 gucuaca   ti pĕra   cada tobi ca
gu-cua=ca-∅   ti pe^{LH}ra cada tobi ca
COMPL-choose=PL-3 a pear   each one DET

'(they) chose a pear each'

50 yendaca   ra   nuu   dxa yaga pĕra
gu-yenda=ca-∅ ra   n-uu   dxa yaga pe^{LH}ra
COMPL-go=PL-3 LOC STAT-be full tree   pear

'(they) went to where the full tree of pears was'

51 ra   dxí'ba   dxa rígola   que
ra   dxi'^{H}ba dxa ri^{H}gola   que^{LH}
LOC climb   full old.man DIST

'where the man was up on'

52 rígola   que   lá
ri^{H}gola   que^{LH} la^{H}
old.man DIST   LA

'that man'

53 ŏraquepe   má   biete   de   lu   yaga quĕ
o^{LH}raquepe ma^{H} bi-ete=∅   de   lu   yaga que^{LH}
when   already COMPL-go.down=3SG from face tree   DIST

'when (he) came down from that tree'

54 lu   ti yaga cue nĭ
lu   ti yaga cue' ni^{LH}
face a tree   side 3SG.INAN

'on the side of the trunk of the tree'

55 raque   bíete
raque^{LH} biete=∅
then   COMPL-go.down=3SG

'then (he) came down'

56 ŏra   biiya   lá
   o^{LH}ra bi-iya=∅   la^H
   when COMPL-see=3SG LA

   'when (he) saw'

57 cayaadxa ti dxumi   pĕrá   stĭ
   ca-yaadxa' ti dxumi^{LH} pe^{LH}ra sti^{LH}=∅
   PROG-miss a basket   pear   POSS=3SG

   'a basket of his pears was missing'

58 que   gánna   tu   la   gucua   ni   nĭ
   que^{LH} g-anna=∅ tu^H la^{LH} gu-cua   ni^{LH} ni^{LH}
   NEG   POT-know who name COMPL-grab 3   3SG.INAN

   'he didn't know who grabbed it'

59 biiyadxisibe   guiónna' badunguiuhuiini quĕ
   bi-iyadxisi^{LH}=be^{LH}   guio^Hnna' badunguiiu-huiini que^{LH}
   COMPL-see.fixedly-only=3SG third   boy-DIM   DIST

   'he looked fixedly at those three little kids'

60 ŏra   gudí'dica   ra nuubĕ
   o^{LH}ra gu-di'^Hdi=ca-∅   ra n-uu=be^{LH}
   when COMPL-pass=PL-3 LOC STAT-be=3SG

   'when (they) passed by where he was'

61 ne   [guza-] gúdí'dica
   ne^{LH} [guza-] gu-di'^Hdi=ca-∅
   and   COMPL-pass=PL-3

   'and (they) passed'

62 zĕca   ti neza quĕ
   ze^{LH}=ca-∅   ti neza que^{LH}
   PROG.go=PL-3 a path DIST

   '(they) went on that path'

63 laabe qué ñannabe   tú lá gucua dxumi pĕrá
  laa=be^{LH} que ñ-anna=be^{LH} tu la gucua dxumi^{LH} pe^{LH}ra
  BASE=3SG NEG IRR-know=3SG who name COMPL-pick basket pear
  stĭbĕ
  sti^{LH}=be^{LH}
  POSS=3SG

  'he would not know who took his basket of pears'

Appendix B

T: 001 dxi que   nalasébě
     dxi que^{LH} nalase'^{H}=be^{H}
     day DEM   thin=3SG.HUM

     'Back then he was thin'

002 laabe   lá
     laa=be^{LH} la^{H}
     BASE=3SG.HUM LA

     'as for him'

003 ma   biiyabe
     ma'^{H} bi-iya=be^{LH}
     already COMPL-see=3SG.HUM

     'he already saw'

004 bia'
     bia'
     about

     'about'

005 bia'   nalasébě
     bia'   na-lase'^{H}=bebe^{LH}
     about STAT-thin=3SG.HUM

     'he was pretty thin'

006 nalasébě
     na-lase'^{H}=be^{LH}
     STAT-thin=3SG.HUM

     'he was thin'

007 nabé   nalasébě
nabe^H na-lase'^{H}=be^{LH}
very   STAT-thin=3SG.HUM

'he was very thin'

M: 008 dxi que   nuá   Měxico mecánico   laabě
dxi que^{LH} n-uu^{LH}=a'^{H} Měxico meca^{LH}nico laa=be^{LH}
day DIST   STAT-to.be=1SG Mexico mechanic   BASE=3SG.HUM

'Back then I was a mechanic in Mexico City'

009 xcuidihuiini   xa
xcuidi-huiini' xa
child-DIM   INTJ

'a child'

010 muchachuhuiini'
muchachu-huiini'
young.man-DIM

'a young man'

011 dxi bixooňé   ja
dxi bixooňe'   ja
day COMPL-run-a'^{H} INTJ

'when I ran, huh'

012 maratón   internacional que   lá
maratón   internacional que^{LH} la^H
marathon international DIST   LA

'the international marathon,'

T: 013 aja
aja
yeah

'Yeah'

M: 014 ¿xi   lanĭ?
      xi   la=ni^LH
      what name=3SG.INAN

      'What was it called?'

015 má   nápá   veintidós   iza
    ma'^H   na-apa=a'^H   veintidos^H   iza
    already STAT-have=1SG twenty-two year

    'I was already 22 years old'

016 veintidós   iza   napá   dxi quĕ
    veintidos^H   iza   na-apa=a'^H   dxi que^LH
    twenty-two year STAT-have=1SG day DIST

    'I was 22 years old then'

017 lu novĕnta-y-dos
    lu novĕnta-y-dos
    PP ninety-two

    'in '92'

018 lu iza   novĕnta-y-dos
    lu iza   novĕnta-y-dos
    PP year ninety-two

    'in the year '92'

019 pĕro   nagasi   má   nuunu   dós mil   dŏce
    pe^LHro nagasi^LH ma^H   n-uu=nu^LH   dos mil   do^LHce
    but   now   already STAT-be=1PL.INCL two thousand twelve

    'but now it's already 2012'

T: 020 ¿ma   panda   íza?
       ma'^H   panda^LH   iza
       already how.many year

       'How many years ago?'

M: 021 gandě
gande^{LH}
twenty

'Twenty'

T: 022 ma   bia'   gande íza
ma   bia'   gande^{LH} iza
already about twenty year

'Already about twenty years'

M: 023 má   raca   gande íza
ma'^H   raca   gande^{LH} iza
already HAB-occur twenty   year

'It's already been twenty years'

T: 024 ¿pabiá   ti   lidxi que   yá?
pabia'^H   ti   lidxi que^{LH} ya
how.much one house DIST   Q

'How much did a house cost?'

M: 025 bia   nasoolo   namás que jmá nalasé   xa
bia' na-soo=lu'   namas^H que jma^H na-lase'^H=a'^H xa
about STAT-tall=2SG only   that more STAT-thin=1SG INTJ

'I was about the same height, I was just thinner'

026 nalasébé   biá   naa
na-lase'^H=be^{LH}   bia' naa
STAT-thin=3SG.HUM about 1SG

'he was thin like me'

T: 027 ¿panda   íza-
panda^{LH}   iza
how.many year

'How many years'

028 ¿panda   este kílŏmetro   bixooñelu   raquě?
     panda^{LH} este kilo^{LH}metro bi-xooñe=lu'   raque^{LH}
     how.many INTJ kilometer   COMPL-run=2SG then

     'How many, um, kilometers did you run then?'

M: 029 cuarénta-y-dos
     cuare^{H}nta-y-dos
     forty-two

     'Forty-two'

030 cuarénta-y-dos   kilŏmetro
     cuare^{H}nta-y-dos kilo^{LH}metro
     forty-two   kilometer

     'forty-two kilometers'

T: 031 chupa   chónná   gúbidxa zeedandarú   dxi guxooñelu   quě
     chupa^{LH} chonna^{H} gubidxa z-eedanda^{LH}-ru   dxi gu-xooñel=u'   que^{LH}
     two   three   sun   PART=arrive=still day POT-run=2SG DIST

     'Two or three days would pass while you'd be running'

032 ¿bi'nu   xiĭxá   éjércício lá?
     bi-i'ni=lu'   xii^{LH}xa^{LH} ejerci^{H}cio la^{H}
     COMPL-do=2SG something exercise   LA

     'Did you do some exercise?'

033 ¿o laaca casi biasalu   lu cama   zuxooñelu?
     o   laaca casi bi-asa=lu'   lu ca^{LH}ma   zu-xooñe=lu'
     or same as COMPL-get.up=2SG PP FUT-run=2SG

     'Or just as you got out of bed you went to run?

M: 034 pues normál xa
     pues normal^{H} xa
     well normal INTJ

     'Well, normal'

035 ejercício ira dxí
ejerci^{LH}cio guira'^{LH} dxi
PL exercise all

'I did the exercises every day'

T: 036 ¿ma^{LH}cá lá?
ma^{LH}ca^{LH} la^{H}
really LA

'Really?'

M: 037 naa siémpre uxóo ne'
naa siem^{H}pre gu^{LH}-xoo ne=a'
1SG always POT-run=1SG

'I would always run'

038 puro de chii kilŏmetro
puro de chii kilometro
all of ten kilometer

'all ten kilometers'

039 xhono kilŏmetro
xhono kilo^{LH}metro
eight kilometer

'eight kilometers'

T: 040 ¿pabiá uxoóñelu ira dxi ya?
pabia'^{H} gu^{LH}-xooñe=lu guira'^{LH} dxi ya?
hom.much POT-run=2SG all day Q

'How much would you run every day?'

041 ¿chii kilŏmetro ti dxi ruxooño la?
chii kilo^{LH}metro ti dxi ru-xooñe=lu' la^{H}
ten kilometer one day HAB-run=2SG LA

'You would run ten kilometers a day?'

M: 042 siádosǐ
    sia^H do'=si^{LH}
    morning=only

    'Just in the morning'

T: 043 ya aja
    ya aja
    ok yes

    'Ok, yes'

M: 044 guxoǒñé   jaa
    gu^{LH}-xooñe=a'^H jaa
    POT-run=1SG   INTJ

    'I would run, huh'

045 pa   xhónó   kílǒmentro lá
    pa^{LH} xhono^{LH} kilo^{LH}metro la^H
    if   eight   kilometer   LA

    'either eight kilometers'

046 o chii kilometro
    o chii kilo^{LH}metro
    or ten kilometer

    'or ten kilometers'

047 dede a la cínco de la mañǎna   lá
    dede a la ci^H nco de la maña^{LH}na la^H
    PP   at the five PP the morning LA

    'from five in the morning'

048 hasta las séis-y-media de la mañǎna
    hasta las seis^H-y-media de la maña^{LH}na
    PP   the six-thirty   PP the morning

    'until six-thirty in the morning'

149

049 párque   Tezozŏmoc   este
par^{H}que Tezozo^{LH}moc este
park   Tezozomoc   INTJ

'Tezozomoc Park, um,'

050 delegación Azcapotzálco   de la   tabăcalera   buěno
delegacion Azcapotzal^{H}co de la   taba^{LH}calera, bue^{LH}no
district   Azcatpotzalco PP the Tabacalera   well

'Azcapotzalco District in the Tabacalera [neighborhood], well'

T: 051 ah   gaxha de ra   panteón   este
ah   gaxha de ra   panteon^H este
INTJ close   PP LOC mausoleum INTJ

'Ah, close to the mausoleum, um'

M: 052 panteón,   este, panteón   San Isĭdro
panteon^H este panteon^H San Isi^{LH}dro
mausoleum INTJ mausoleum San Isidro

'Mausoleum, um, San Isidro mausoleum'

T: 053 cădi   zitu ndĭ'
ca^{LH}di zitu ndi'^{LH}
NEG   far DEM

'It's not far'

M: 054 cădi   zitu ndĭ'
ca^{LH}di zitu ndi'^{LH}
NEG   far DEM

'It's not far'

057 gaxha de ra   métro   este Rosărio
gaxha de ra   me^{H}tro este Rosa^{LH}rio
close   PP LOC metro   INTJ Rosario

'close to the Rosario metro [station]'

T: 058   mápe   nga   zítu nuŭ   métro   Rosărio
          ma'pe nga^{LH} zitu n-uu^{LH} me^{H}tro Rosa^{LH}rio
          already NGA   far STAT-to.be metro Rosario

          'It's far from the Rosario metro [station]'

M: 059   ya, métro Rosărio   lá
          ya   me^{H}tro Rosa^{LH}rio la^{H}
          INTJ metro Rosario   LA

          'Rosario Metro'

    060   rarĭ'
          rari'^{LH}
          here

          'is here' (gestures with right hand)

    061   ne   pánteón   San Isĭdro   cherĭ'
          ne^{LH} panteon^{H} San Isi^{LH}dro cheri'^{LH}
          and   mausoleum San Isidro   here

          'and San Isidro mausoleum is here' (gestures with left hand)

    062   bia'
          bia'
          about

          'around here'

T: 063   ¿raque bíxoo nelu   panda   kílŏmetro?
          raque^{LH} bi-xooñe=lu'   panda^{LH} kilo^{LH}metro?
          then   COMPL-run=2SG kilometer

          'Then you ran how many kilometers?'

M: 064   co, raque   rárí   gúné'   entrenăr
          co raque^{LH} rari'^{LH} gu-ini=a'^{H} entrenar^{LH}
          no then   here COMPL-do=1SG train

          'No, I trained here'

T: 065 ya
    ya
    ok

    'OK'

066 ¿bixooñelu   raque   pándă?
    bi-xooñe=lu'   raque^{LH} panda^{LH}
    COMPL-run=2SG then   how.many

    'You ran how many?'

M: 067 chupa   kílŏmetro napani   álrededór
    chupa^{LH} kilo^{LH}metro na-apa=ni^{LH} alrededor^{H}
    two   kilometer STAT-have=3SG.INAN around

    'It is two kilometers around'

T: 068 ¿panda   buélta?
    panda^{LH} buel^{H}ta?
    how.many lap

    'How many laps?'

M: 069 pue udieé   ní   tápa buélta nga xhóno kilŏmetro
    pue gu-diee=a'^{H} ni^{LH} tapa buel^{H}ta nga^{LH} xhono^{LH} kilo^{LH}metro
    well COMPL-give=1SG 3SG.INAN four lap   NGA eight   kilometer

    'Well, four laps is eight kilometers'

070 udieé   ní   gáayu lá
    gu-diee=a'^{H} ni^{LH} gaayu' la^{H}
    COMPL-give=1SG 3SG.INAN five   LA

    'five laps,'

071 chii kilŏmetro   xa
    chii kilo^{LH}metro xa
    ten kilometer   INTJ

    'ten kilometers

072 pa   údieé   ní   xhóopá lá
    pa^{LH} gu-diee=a'^{H} ni^{LH} xhoopa' la^H
    if   COMPL-give=1SG 3SG.INAN six   LA

    'if six'

073 nga   dóce kilŏmetro
    nga^{LH} do^{H}ce kilo^{LH}metro
    NGA   twelve kilometer

    'that is twelve kilometers'

T: 074 yannadxi bixooñelu   este lu maratón qué   lá
       yanna-dxi bi-xooñe=lu'   este lu maraton^H que^{LH} la^H
       now-day COMPL-run=2SG INTJ PP marathon DIST   LA

       'Now, when you, um, ran the marathon,"

075 ¿panda   kílŏmetro?
    panda^{LH} kilo^{H}metro?
    how.many kilometer

    'how many kilometers?'

M: 076 cuarénta-y-dos
       cuare^{H}nta-y-dos
       forty-two

       'Forty-two'

077 dxi gúuyá   qué   lá
    dxi gu^{LH}-uuya=a'^{H} que^{LH} la^H
    day POT-see=1SG   DIST   LA

    'when I saw that,'

078 ucaa   diaaga
    gu-caa   diaaga
    COMPL-put ear

    'listen'

079 nacŭbi   jaa   unuá'   Mĕxico
nacu^{LH}bi jaa   gu-unu^{LH}=a'^{H} Me^{LH}xico
new   INTJ COMPL-travel=1SG Mexico

'I had just travelled to Mexico'

080 como raque   uyuu   Vidál   jmá   huaniisĭ
como raque^{LH} gu-yuu   Vidal^{H} jma^{H} huaniisi^{LH}
as   then   COMPL-go Vidal   POT.go=1SG already

'because then Vidal went, he was older'

081 que   bí'nibe   dxíi na nabĕ
que^{H} bi-i'ni=be^{LH} dxiiña na=be^{LH}
NEG COMPL-do=3SG.HUM work   say=3SG.HUM

'he didn't work, he says'

082 uye   Tomás yeganna   láadŭ
gu-e   Tomas^{H} yeganna^{LH} laadu^{LH}
COMPL-go Tomás   POT.visit   BASE=1PL.EXCL

'Tomás came to visit us'

083 uyebe   yéndabe   á-
gu-e=be^{LH} yenda=be^{LH} a-
COMPL-go=3SG.HUM POT.arrive=3SG.HUM a-

'he went to arrive at-'

084 quí gannadiá   pá   tí   lŭnés   lá
qui^{H} g-anna-di=a'^{H} pa^{LH} ti   lu^{LH}nes la^{H}
NEG COMPL-know-NEG=1SG if   one Monday LA

'I don't know if on a Monday,'

085 o pa   tí   dómíngo
o pa^{LH} ti   domi^{H}ngo
or if   one Sunday

'or if on a Sunday'

086 o éntre sema^{LH}na
o en^{H}tre semana
or between week

‘or in the middle of the week’

087 má zĕdá maratón
ma’^{H} zee^{LH}da^{H} maraton^{H}
already FUT.come marathon

‘the marathon would come soon’

088 pa láabé yéndábe raque lúnes lá
pa^{LH} laa=be^{LH} yenda=be^{LH} raque^{LH} lu^{LH}nes la^{H}
if BASE=3SG.HUM COMPL=3SG.HUM then Monday LA

‘if he came then Monday’

089 o márte
o mar^{H}tes
or Tuesday

‘or Tuesday’

090 domíngo que lá
domi^{H}ngo que^{LH} la^{H}
Sunday DIST LA

‘that Sunday’

091 ngá má ra nga márátón
nga^{H} ma’^{H} ra nga^{LH} maraton^{H}
DEM already LOC NGA marathon

‘that was already when the marathon was’

092 domíngo que ún veintiséis de abríl
domi^{H}ngo que^{LH} un veintiseis^{H} de abril^{H}
Sunday DIST a twenty-six of April

‘Sunday, a twenty-sixth of April’

093 veintiséis   lá
     veintiseis^{H} la^{H}
     twenty-six LA

     'twenty-six'

094 o veintidós   de abríl   pue
     o veintidos^{H} de abril^{LH} pues
     or twenty-two of April   well

     'or, well, twenty-two of April'

095 yendabe   México
     yenda=be^{LH} Me^{H}xico
     COMPL.arrive=3SG.HUM Mexico

     'he arrived in Mexico'

096 para, jaa, cayuidu   díidxa pues
     para jaa ca-ui'=du^{LH} diidxa' pues
     for   INTJ PROG-speak=1PL.EXCL word   well

     'for, well, us to talk'

097 como riuuladxibe   guébé   lá
     como ri-uu-la'dxi'=be^{LH} guebe^{LH} la^{H}
     as   HAB-enter-liver=3SG.HUM POT-drink=3SG.HUM LA

     'because he likes to drink'

098 para bedandădú   Sbado   quě
     para bi-edanda^{LH}du^{LH} Sa^{H}bado que^{LH}
     for   COMPL-arrive.here=1PL.EXCL Saturday DIST

     'for us to arrive that Saturday'

099 bini   citárcabe   láadǔ
     bi-ini   citar^{H}=ca=be^{LH} laa=du^{LH}
     COMPL-do make.appointment=PL=3SG.HUM BASE=1PL.EXCL

     'they made the appointment for us'

100 chuudu   tí   reunión
     chuudu^{LH} ti   reunion^{H}
     POT.go=1PL.EXCL one meeting

     'we went to a meeting'

101 ra jaa Hotél Camĭno Reál, México
     ra jaa Hotel^{H} Cami^{H}no Real^{H} Me^{H}xico
     LOC INTJ Hotel Camino Real Mexico

     'at the Camino Real Hotel, Mexico City'

102 bidii   gueela chuudu   Hotél Camĭno Reál
     bi-dii   gueela' chuu=du^{H} Hotel^{H} Cami^{H}no Real^{H}
     COMPL-give night POT.go=1PL.EXCL Hotel Camino Real

     'night came we went to the Camino Real Hotel

103 bidiicabe   náa ti   playérá   lá
     bi-dii=ca=be^{LH} naa ti   playe^{LH}ra la^{H}
     COMPL-give=PL=3SG.HUM 1SG one shirt   LA

     'they gave me a shirt,'

104 ne   nŭmero
     ne^{LH} nu^{LH}mero
     and number

     'and a number'

105 ne   nŭmero lá
     ne^{LH} nu^{LH}mero la^{H}
     and number LA

     'and a number,'

106 para racă   identificár
     para raca   identificar^{H}
     for HAB-occur identify

     'to identify [us]'

107 nvúmero   maizěna
    nu^{LH}mero maize^{LH}na
    number   Maizena

'number Maizena'

108 de ti,   este, ¿xi   mǒdó nguě?
    de ti,   este, xi^{LH} modo ngue^{LH}
    of one INTJ what way   DEM

'of a, um, what is that?

T: 109 ti   diidxa'
      ti   diidxa'
      one word

'a word'

M: 110 ti   plática   biucabě
      ti   pla^{H}tica   bi-uu=ca=be^{LH}
      one conversation COMPL-enter=PL=3SG.HUM

'a conversation'

111 casi ti   entrenamiěnto
    casi ti   entrenamie^{LH}nto
    like one training

'like a training session'

112 péru   ti   dxi ǎnte
    pe^{LH}ru ti   dxi a^{LH}nte
    but   one day before

'but one day before'

113 viěrne   huaxhinni que   lá
    vie^{LH}rne huaxhinni que^{LH} la^{H}
    Friday   evening   DEM   LA

'that Friday evening'

114 uxudxidǔ
     gu=xudxi=du^{LH}
     COMPL=drink=1PL.EXCL

     'we got drunk'

115 laabe   lá
     laa=be^{LH} la^{H}
     base=3SG.ANIM LA

     'him (pointing)'

116 Vidal lá
     Vidal la^{H}
     Vidal LA

     'Vidal'

117 ne   náa
     ne^{LH} naa
     and   1SG

     'and I'

118 bide'du   jmá   cáguǎma
     bi-de'=du^{LH} jma^{H} cagua^{LH}ma
     COMPL-drink=1PL.EXCL much beer

     'we drank lots of beer'

119 hasta ti   botélla   de bacardí bide'du   ráquě
     hasta ti   bote^{LH}lla de bacardí^{H} bi-de'=du^{LH} raque^{LH}
     even one bottle   of Bacardi COMPL-drink=1PL.EXCL then

     'we even drank a bottle of Bacardi'

120 bira   guéela sǎbado   quě
     bi-ra^{LH} gueela' sa^{LH}bado que^{LH}
     COMPL-end night   Saturday DIST

     'Saturday at dawn'

121 guye   cǐta qué
    gu-e=a'   cita que^H
    COMPL-e=1SG date NEG

    'I went to the appointment'

122 chaǎ
    chaa^{LH}
    POT.go=1SG

    'I go'

123 qui   úyédiá'   dxiiña
    que^{LH} gu-e-di=a'^{H} dxiiña
    NEG   COMPL-go-NEG=1SG work

    'I didn't even go to work'

124 naxudxeruá'
    naxudxerua'
    STAT-drunk-still=1SG

    'I was still drunk'

125 yendayá'
    gu-enda=a'^{H}
    COMPL-arrive=1SG

    'when I arrived'

126 para bira   guéela bicaacabé   lá
    para bi-ra^{LH} gueela' bi-caa=ca=be^{LH} la^H
    for   COMPL-end night   COMPL-put=PL=3SG.HUM LA

    'for when the night ended, they called'

127 ne   gúdxi   que raca   uleza   stale stálé bínní úye
    ne^{LH} gu-dxi   que r-aca   uleza   stale^{LH} stale^{LH} binni^{LH} gu-e
    and   COMPL-say that HAB-occur COMPL-wait many   many   people   COMPL-go

    'and it was said that many many people were expected to come'

128	stale	stálě
	stale^{LH}	stale^{LH}
	many	many

'many many'

139	míles
	mil^{H}es
	thousands

'thousands'

130	para	nuá	xa
	para	n-uu^{LH}=a'^{H}	xa
	for	STAT-to.be=1SG.HUM	INTJ

'for me there,'

131	pues	naa	lá
	pues	naa	la^{H}
	well	1SG	LA

'well as for me,'

132	pues	uyé	nörmál	xa
	pues	gu-e=a'^{H}	normal^{H}	xa
	well	COMPL-go=1SG	normal	INTJ

'well I went, normal'

133	zaca,	dé	pantalń	mezclílla	zacă
	zaca^{LH}	de	pantalon^{H}	mezcli^{H}lla	zaca^{LH}
	that.way	PP	pants	jean	that.way

'that way, with jean pants'

134	ira	ní	gúye	que	lá
	guira'^{LH}	ni^{LH}	guye	que^{LH}	la^{H}
	all	REL	COMPL-go	DIST	LA

'all the ones that went'

135 pŭro   de pánts   laaca xa
$pu^{LH}ro$ de $pan^{H}ts$ laaca xa
all   PP pants   also   INTJ

'only in athletic pants'

136 ŏjo,   pŭro   profesionál
$o^{LH}jo$ $pu^{LH}ro$ $profesional^{H}$
INTJ   all   professional

'wow, all professionals'

137 pŭro   de pánts   tĕnis   jaa
$pu^{LH}ro$ de $pan^{H}ts$ $te^{LH}nis$ jaa
all   PP pants   tennis.shoes INTJ

'all in athletic pants, tennis shoes, huh'

138 tĕnis   qué   zínié'
$te^{LH}nis$ que^{H} $zi\text{-}ne^{LH}=a^{,H}$
tennis.shoes NEG   FUT-bring=1SG

'I didn't bring tennis shoes'

139 pero ziniá   pantalón   de mezclílla
pero $zi\text{-}ne^{LH}=a^{,H}$ $pantalon^{LH}$ de $mezcli^{LH}lla$
but   FUT-bring=1SG

'but I brought jeans'

140 ŏra   biiyá   lá
$o^{LH}ra$ $bi\text{-}uuya=a^{,H}$ la^{H}
when COMPL-see=1SG LA

'when I saw'

141 biiya   ca binni   qué   né   pánts   támbién
$bi\text{-}uuya=a^{,H}$ ca $binni^{LH}$ que^{LH} ne^{LH} $pants^{H}$ $tambien^{H}$
COMPL-see=1SG PL person   DIST   and   pants   also

'I saw the people with pants also'

142 peru qué   gunebia'ya'diá   laacabě
      peru que^{H} gu-nebia'ya'-di=a'^{H} laacabe^{LH}
      but   COMPL-know-NEG=1SG BASE=PL=3.HUM

'but I didn't know them at all'

T: 143 má   guxudxilu'   jaa
      ma'^{H} gu-xudxi=lu'   jaa
      already COMPL-drunk=2SG INTJ

'You were already drunk huh'

M: 144 stale   bínní   núu   stálě
      stale^{LH} binni^{LH} n-uu^{LH} stale^{LH}
      many   person STAT-to.be many

'Many, many people there'

T: 145 ah   pues si   ¿candá   cérvěza   ruaalu'   ya?
      ah   pues si   ca-nda'   cerve^{LH}za ruaa=lu'   ya
      INTJ well yes PROG-smell beer   mouth=2SG Q

'Well, yeah, your mouth was smelling like beer huh?'

M: 146 stale   bínní   núu   ráquě
      stale^{LH} binni^{LH} n-uu^{LH} raque^{LH}
      many   person STAT-to.be then

'There were many people then'

T: 147 stale   xhó   nuu   ruáalu'
      stale^{LH} xho' n-uu^{LH} ruaalu'
      many   smell STAT-to.be mouth=2SG

'Many smells in your mouth'

M: 148 stale   bádudxaapa
      stale^{LH} badudxaapa
      many   girl

'Many women'

149 stale bádunguiiu
    stale^H badunguiiu
    many boy

    'many men'

150 de iră'-
    de guira'^{LH}
    PP all

    'of all-'

151 aja, de ira   cláse
    aja de guira'^{LH} cla^{H}se
    yes PP all   kind

    'of all kinds'

152 de ira   médĭda
    de guira'^{LH} medi^{LH}da
    PP all   sizes

    'of all sizes'

153 peru ara guyuŭdú   lá
    peru ara gu-uu^{LH}=du^{LH} la^H
    but   now COMPL-to.be=1PL.EXCL LA

    'but now we are there,'

154 para bidiicabe   láadú   lá
    para bidiicabe^{LH} laadu^{LH} la^H
    for   COMPL-give=PL=3.HUM LAA=1PL.EXCL LA

    'for them to give us,'

155 ti   número   lá
    ti   nu^{LH}mero la^{LH}
    one number   LA

    'a number'

156 ne   tí   pláyĕra
ne^{LH} ti playe^{LH}ra
and   one shirt

'and a shirt'

157 ŏraque   lá
o^{LH}raque^{LH} la^{H}
now   LA

'then,'

158 bisiga'de   que lá
bi-siga'de' que^{LH} la^{H}
COMPL-give DIST   LA

'that was given'

159 ŏra ti paquété lá
o^{LH}ra ti paque^{H}te la^{LH}
when one package

'when a package'

160 bisiga'de   maizĕná   lá
bi-siga'de' maize^{LH}na la^{H}
COMPL-give Maizena   LA

'Maizena was given'

161 ti   naga'nda Espráit
ti   naga'nda Esprait^{H}
one STAT-cold Sprite

'a Sprite soda'

162 bini   patrocinár Coca Cŏla
bi-i'ni patrocinar^{H} Coca Co^{LH}la
COMPL-do sponsor   Coca Cola

'Coca Cola sponsored (the event)'

163 Espráit lá
Esprait^H la^H
Sprite LA

'Sprite'

164 chupa máizĕná lá
chupa^{LH} maize^{LH}na la^H
two Maizena LA

'two Maizena'

165 ma nguesi zulua'
ma'^{LH} ngue-si^{LH} z-ulu=a'^H
already DEM- FUT-believe=1SG

'that's it, I think'

166 peru lá
peru la^H
but LA

'but'

167 ze ti bólsa ti paquéte pue
z-e ti bol^Hsa ti paque^Hte pues
FUT-go one bag one package well

'there came a bag, well, a package

168 ah ne zeĕda gadxe revísta raquĕ
ah ne^{LH} z-ee^{LH}da gadxe revi^Hsta raque^{LH}
INTJ and FUT-come different magazine then

'and there came a different magazine'

169 revísta de corredŏré lănĭ
revis^Hta de corredo^{LH}res la'^{LH}=ni
magazine Corredores name=3SG.INAN

'its name is Corredores (Runners) magazine'

170 casi ti   libru pue
     casi ti   libru pues
     like one book well

     '(It's) like a book'

171 informaciń   ne   nĭ
     informacion^{H} ne^{LH} ni^{LH}
     information   with 3SG.INAN

     'with information'

172 ne   zeĕda   ti   jaa ti   plănu
     ne^{LH} z-ee^{LH}da ti jaa ti pla^{LH}nu
     and   FUT-come one INTJ one map

     'and there came a map'

173 ti   plănú   lá
     ti   pla^{LH}nu la^{H}
     one map   LA

     'a "planu"'

174 o ti   mápa
     o ti   ma^{H}pa
     or one map

     'or a "mapa"'

175 iră   ní   pue para información
     guira'^{LH} ni^{LH} pues para informacion^{H}
     all   3SG.INAN well for   information

     'well, all of it for information'

176 para săbado
     para sa^{LH}bado
     for   Saturday

     'for Saturday'

177 domíngo que lá
    domi^{H}ngo que^{LH} la^H
    Sunday DIST LA

    'on Sunday'

178 domíngo siádo'   que lá
    domi^{H}ngo sia^{H}do' que^{LH} la^H
    Sunday   morning DIST LA

    'on Sunday morning,'

179 pue como nayaa   nuá   qué lá,
    pues como nayaa   n-uu^{LH}=a$^{'H}$ que^{LH} la^H
    well as   STAT-raw STAT-to.be=1SG DIST LA

    'because I was hungover'

180 cădi   nada'na'   endaro' xa
    ca^{LH}di na-da'na' endaro' xa
    NEG   STAT-tempt food   INTJ

    'food wasn't appetizing'

181 má   candaaná   gueela'
    ma$^{'H}$ ca-ndaana=a$^{'H}$ gueela'
    already PROG-be.hungry=1SG night

    'I started to be hungry at night'

182 udahuá   normál
    gu-dahua$^{H'}$ normal^H
    COMPL-eat.1SG normal

    'I ate normal (as I normally would)'

183 normál udahuá'
    normal^H gu-dahua'^{H}
    normal COMPL-eat.1SG

    'I ate NORMAL (as I normally would) '

184 pero domíngo siádo   dxi maratón qué   lá
    pero domi^{H}ngo sia^{H}do' dxi maraton^H que^{LH} la^H
    but Sunday   morning day marathon DIST LA

    'but on Sunday morning on the day of the marathon'

185 ánte   de las ocho chuudu   pendiente
    an^{H}te de las ocho ch-uu=du^{LH} pendien^{H}te
    before PP the eight POT-go=1PL.EXCL matter

    'before 8 o'clock we had a place to be'

186 bira   géela domíngo
    bi-ra^{LH} gueela' domi^{H}ngo
    COMPL-end night   Sunday

    'Sunday at dawn'

187 bibané   lá
    bi-bani=a'^{H} la^H
    COMPL-wake.up=1SG LA

    'I woke up,'

188 guzé   xa
    gu-zi=a'^{H} xa
    COMPL-shower=1SG INTJ

    'I showered,'

189 güé   ti jŭgo de narănjasi   xá
    gü-e-a'^{H} ti ju^{LH}go de nara^{LH}nja-si^{LH} xa
    COMPL-drink=1SG one juice of orange-only   INTJ

    'I drank an orange juice only.'

190 pero naa lá
    pero naa la
    but 1SG LA

    'but I,'

191 rabé   fácilni   xá
r-abi=a'^{H} fa^{H}cil=ni^{LH} xa
HAB-say=1SG easy=3SG.INAN INTJ

'I say it was easy'

192 osĕa   nagueendani   pué
ose^{LH}a na-gueenda-ni^{LH} pues
SO   STAT-fast=3SG.INAN well

'well, it was fast'

193 qué ñuné'   este pensárdiá   de que pa   zítúnǐ
que^H ñ-uni=a'^{LH} este pensar^{LH}-di=a'^{H} de que pa^{LH} zitu=ni^{LH}
NEG IRR-do=1SG um think-NEG=1SG PP that if   far=3SG.INAN

'I didn't even think whether it was far'

194 ŏra   guyuudu   qué   xá
o^{LH}ra guyuudu^{LH} que^{LH} xa
when COMPL-go=1PL.EXCL DIST   INTJ

'the time we went'

195 má   gundaa   las ocho
ma'^{H} gu-ndaa   las ocho
already COMPL-be.late the eight

'already after eight'

196 má   cayete   tutiiisí   qué lá
ma'^{H} ca-ete   tutii^{LH}si^{LH} que^{LH} la^H
already PROG-fall everyone DIST LA

'already everyone had fallen'

197 qué uyuti   jaa
que^H gu-ati   jaa
NEG COMPL-die INTJ

'not dead, huh'

198 pue casi ca gunaa   que   xa
    pues casi ca guaa   que^{LH} xa
    well like PL woman DIST   INTJ

'well, like the women,'

199 pantalón   de mezclïlla
    pantalon^H de mezcli^{LH}lla
    pants   of jeans

'jean pants'

200 ŏraque   sié   lá
    o^{LH}raque^{LH} si=a'^{H} la^H
    now   COMPL.buy=1SG LA

'now I bought'

201 ti   shórt
    ti   short^H
    one short

'shorts'

202 sié   ti   par těnis
    si=a'^{H} ti   par te^{LH}nis
    COMPL.buy=1SG one pair tennis.shoes

'I bought a pair of tennis shoes'

203 írútí   qué   runebia'yá
    gui^{H}ru^{H}ti'^{H} que^H r-unebia'=a'^{H}
    nobody   NEG   HAB-know=1SG

'I didn't know anyone'

204 stubé'
    stubi^{LH}=a'^{H}
    alone

'I was alone'

205 peru ŏra   bira   guéela lá
     peru o^{LH}ra bira^{LH} gueela' la^{H}
     but when COMPL-end night LA

     'but at dawn'

206 vuélta jŭgo de   narănja nguésí   güé   pue
     vuel^{H}ta ti   ju^{LH}go de   nara^{LH}nja ngue^{LH}-si^{LH} gu-e=a'^{H} pues
     again juice of   orange DEM-   COMPL-drink=1SG well

     'again, well, I drank just an orange juice'

207 nin   quí ñahuadiá   de endaré   gastí'
     nin   qui ñ-ahua-di=a'^{H} de guendaro=a'^{H} gasti'^{H}
     not.even NEG IRR-eat/drink-NEG=1SG of food=1SG   nothing

     'I didn't even eat/drink any of my food'

208 jŭgo   quesí   güé'
     ju^{LH}go que^{LH}-si^{LH} gu-e=a'^{H}
     juice DEM-only COMPL-eat/drink=1SG

     'I drank only the juice.'

209 iza   má   stale bínní xa
     ri-iza   ma'^{LH} stale^{LH} binni^{LH} xa
     HAB-walk already many person INTJ

     'many people were walking'

210 cuzeetecabe   lú sonĭdo   quě
     cu-zeete=ca=be^{LH} lu soni^{LH}do que^{LH}
     PROG-mention=PL=3SG.HUM PP sound   DIST

     'they mentioned that on the sound system'

211 cuzeetecabe   íra   ni   chúxooñe ca   lá
     cu-zeete=ca=be^{LH} guira'^{LH} ni^{LH} chu-xooñe ca   la^{H}
     cu-zeete=ca=be^{LH} all   REL POT-run   DEM LA

     'they mentioned all those who were going to run'

212 zuhuaacabě en fila lá,
  zuhuaa=ca=be^{LH} en fila la^H
  FUT.stand=PL=3SG.HUM in line LA

  'they were all standing in line'

213 purtí má las ocho de la mañǎna chuzulu
  purti'^H ma'^{LH} las ocho de la maña^{LH}na chu-zulu
  because already the eight of the morning POT-begin

  'because it would begin at eight in the morning'

214 chi guiaaxha ca binni cá chuxooñeca
  chi gui^{LH}-aaxha ca binni^{LH} ca chu-xooñe=ca=∅
  POT POT-start PL person DEM POT-run=PL=3

  'the people would begin to run'

215 ¿pabiá', este, cayuninacabe lá,
  pabia'^H este ca-uni-na=ca=be^{LH} la^H
  how.much INTJ PROG-do-say=PL=3SG.HUM LA

  'How many, um, were they saying'

216 chuxooñe?
  chu-xooñe?
  POT-run

  'would run?'

217 unaa ne jáa hǒmbre lá,
  gunaa ne^{LH} jaa hombre la
  woman and INTJ man LA

  'Women and men,"

218 nacabe cá unaa ca lá
  na=ca=be^{LH} ca gunaa ca la^H
  say=PL=3SG.HUM PL woman DEM LA

  'they say the women,'

219 ziaaxhaca   primér nacabĕ
    z-iaaxha=ca=Ø primer^H na=ca=be^H
    FUT-start=PL=3 first   say=PL=3SG.HUM

    'they started first'

220 tonce ca hŏmbre   ca lá,
    tonce ca ho^{LH}mbre ca la^H
    then PL man   DEM LA

    'so the men,'

221 pues rarirópa
    pues rariro^{H}pa
    well second

    'well, second'

222 tonce ca ni   má   ca huaxooñe ca lá,
    tonce ca ni^{LH} ma'^{H} ca hua-xooñe ca   la
    then PL REL already PL PERF-run DEM LA

    'so those who had already run,'

223 chuu   delánte
    chuu   dela^{H}nte
    POT-go front

    'would go in front'

224 ni   jmá qué huaxooñe que   lá,
    ni^{LH} jma^H que^H hua-xooñe que^{LH} la
    PL   REL   more NEG   PERF-run DIST LA

    'the majority who had not run,'

225 chuu   de atrás
    chuu   de atras^H
    POT-go PP back

    'would go in back'

T: 226 ¿xi mŏdo?
xi^{LH} mo^{LH}do?
what way

'In what way?

M: 227 peru ŏraque cáyaca colocár ira bínni qué pue
peru o^{LH}raque^{LH} ca-aca colocar^H guira'^{LH} binni^{LH} que^{LH} pue
but then PROG-occur place all person DIST INTJ

'But then all the people were placed,"

228 nuu dé ira cláse,
nuu^{LH} de guira' cla^{H}se
DIST INTJ STAT-to.be of all

'there were many different types'

229 nuu dé ira médĭda
nuu^{LH} de guira'^{LH} medi^{LH}da
STAT-to.be of all size

'they were of all sizes'

230 ira núu huániisi también ya
guira'^{LH} nuu^{LH} huaniisi^{LH} tambien^H ya
all STAT-to.be older also INTJ

'all were older also'

231 peru iza stale bínnĭ
peru iza stale^{LH} binni^{LH}
but POT-to.walk many person

'but many people went'

232 zuluasiá quince míl
z-ulua-si=a'^{H} quince mil^H
FUT-think-even=1SG fifteen thousand

'I think fifteen thousand'

175

233 quínce míl   participánte parecesi lá,
    quin^Hce mil^H   participan^Hte parece-si^H la^H
    fifteen thousand participants   seem-only LA

'about fifteen thousand only'

234 o diesisés   míl
    o diesiseis^H mil^H
    or sixteen   thousand

'or sixteen thousand'

T: 235 ¿pero cuarenta-y-dós kilŏmetro   bixooñelu   lá?
       pero cuarenta-y-dos^H kilo^{LH}metro bi-xooñe=lu'   la^H?
       but   forty-two   kilometer COMPL-run=2SG LA

'But you ran forty-two kilometers?'

M: 236 ya, bixooñé'
        ya, bi-xooñe=a'^H
        yes COMPL-run=1SG

'Yes, I ran'

237 sti   dxi que   lá
    sti   dxi que^{LH} la^H
    other day DIST   LA

'the next day,'

238 chi   guné   dxiiña
    chi   gu^{LH}-i'ni=a'^H dxiiña
    POT.go POT-do=1SG   work

'I went to work'

239 ti   semăna   gutá'
    ti   sema^{LH}na gu=ta=a'^H
    one week   COMPL-lay.down=1SG

'I laid down one week'

240 zacá nachonga ñée'
  zaca^{LH} nachonga ñee=a'^{H}
  that.way STAT-stiff leg=1SG

  'my leg was stiff like this'

241 cádi chicharrónchonga
  ca^{H}di chicharron^H-chonga
  NEG pork.rind-stiff

  'not a stiff pork rind'

242 ŏra biluxe maratón que lá
  o^{LH}ra bi-luxe maraton^H que^{LH} la^H
  when COMPL-end marathon DIST LA

  'when the marathon ended,'

243 chonna ŏra ne cuárénta y tanto minŭto bixooñé nǐ
  chonna^{LH} o^{LH}ra ne^{LH} cuare^{H}nta- y-tanto minu^{LH}to bi-xooñe=a'^{H} ni^{LH}
  three hour and forty- some minute COMPL-run=1SG 3SG.INAN

  'I ran it in three hours forty-some minutes'

244 ¿tu bíni ganár ní?
  tu^{LH} bi-i'ni ganar^H ni^{LH}
  who COMPL-do win 3SG.INAN

  'who won it?'

245 chupa ŏra ne quínce minútó lá,
  chupa^{LH} o^{LH}ra ne^{LH} qui^{H}nce minu^{H}to la^H
  two hour and fifteen minute LA

  'two hours and fifteen minutes'

246 chupa ŏra ne gándé mínúto zuluá'
  chupa^{LH} o^{LH}ra ne^{LH} gande^{LH} minu^{H}to zulu=a'^{H}
  two hour and twenty minute FUT.believe

  'I think two hours and twenty minutes'

247 badudxaapa que   lá
   badudxaapa que^{LH} la^H
   woman   DIST LA

'the woman,'

248 mexicána   ca   lá
   mexica^{H}na ca   la^H
   Mexican   DEM LA

'the Mexican [runner],'

249 laaca chupa   ŏrá   lá
   laaca chupa^{LH} o^{LH}ra la^H
   also two   hour LA

'also two hours'

250 peru jmá   minúto
   peru jma^H minu^{H}to
   but more minute

'but more minutes'

251 casi chonna ora   zulua'
   casi chonna ora   zulu=a'^{H}
   like three   hour FUT.believe=1SG

'almost three hours I think'

252 naa lá
   naa la^H
   1SG LA

'as for me'

253 pue casi tapa ŏra
   pues casi tapa o^{LH}ra
   well like four hour

'well, about four hours'

254 ŏra   biiyá   stale bínní zéeda   lá
o^{LH}ra bi-uuya=a'^H   stale^{LH} binni^H z-eeda   la^H
when COMPL-see=1SG many   person FUT-arrive LA

'when I saw many people arrive'

255 zeeda   badunguiiu badudxaapa
z-eeda   badunguiiu badudxaapa
FUT-arrive man   woman

'men, women arrived'

256 zaca   rúlui   biri laaca   zeedaca
zaca^{LH}   ru-lui   biri laa=ca=∅ z-eeda=ca=∅
that.way HAB-show ant   BASE=PL=3 FUT-arrive=PL=3

'that way they seemed like ants as they were arriving'

257 buěnu   ti   semăna   gutá'
bue^{LH}nu ti   sema^{LH}na guta=a'^H
well   one week   COMPL-lay.down=1SG

'well, I laid down for one week'

258 que^H gandá   saa
que^H g-anda=a'^{LH}   saa
NEG   COMPL-be.able=1SG party

'I couldn't go to any parties'

259 guira   dxí cadaabiá'
guira'^{LH} dxi ca-daabi=a'^{LH}
all   day PROG-massage=1SG

'I massaged myself every day'

260 bidiicabe   náa ti   medălla
bi-dii=ca=be^{LH}   naa ti   meda^{LH}lla
COMPL-give=PL=3SG.HUM 1SG one medal

'they gave me a medal'

261 ira   ní   yénda   lu métá lá

guira'^{LH} ni^{LH} yenda   lu me^{H}ta la^{H}

all   REL arrive.here PP goal LA

'everyone that arrived at the finish line'

262 cuacani

cua=ca=ni^{LH}

grab=PL=3SG.INAN

'got one'

263 yanna má   quí udxela   foto quě

yanna ma   qui gu-dxela   foto que

now   already NEG COMPL-find-1SG DIST

'now I can't find the photo'

264 qui   gápa   foto stinné'

qui^{LH} g-apa   foto stinne=a'^{H}

NEG COMPL-have photo mine

'I didn't have my picture'

265 ¿tu lá   bini   ganár, este, primér lugár?

tu^{LH} la^{LH} b-ini   ganar^{H} este primer^{H} lugar^{H}

who name COMPL-do win   INTJ first   place

'Who won, um, first place?'

266 ti   militár bini   ganár dxiquě

ti   militar^{H} b̦i-ini   ganar^{H} dxique^{LH}

one soldier COMPL-do win   then

'a soldier won then'

267 naa quí ñapadiá   entrenadór

naa qui^{H} ñ-apa-di=a'^{H} entrenador^{H}

1SG NEG IRR-have-NEG=1SG trainer

'I didn't have a trainer'

268 quí   ñápá'
qui^H ñapa=a'^{H}
NEG IRR-have=1SG

'I didn't have'

269 naa stubesiá'
naa stube-si=a'^{H}
1SG alone=only=1SG

'it was just me'

270 huati   quě
huati^{LH} que^H
dumb   DIST

'that was dumb'

271 ngá   nga   rúxooñe
nga^H nga^{LH} ru-xooñe
DEM NGA HAB-run

'that's what it is to run'

272 peru ruxooñe riésgo
peru ruxooñe ries^{H}go
but HAB-run risk

'but to run a risk'

References

Alfabeto popular para la escritura del zapoteco del Istmo. 1956. Mexico City, Mexico: Sociedad Pro-Planeación Integral del Istmo; El Consejo de Lenguas Indígenas; El Instituto Lingüístico de Verano.

Arellanes, Francisco. 2009. *El sistema fonológico y las propiedades fonéticas del zapoteco de San Pablo Güilá: Descripción y análisis formal.* El Colegio de México dissertation.

Ariel, Mira. 1988. Referring and accessibility. *Journal of Linguistics* 24(1). 65–87.

Ariel, Mira. 1990. *Accessing noun-phrase antecedents.* New York: Routledge.

Ariel, Mira. 2001. Accessibility theory: An overview. In Ted Sanders, Joost Schilperoord & Wilbert Spooren (eds.), *Text representation: Linguistic and psycholinguistic aspects*, 29–87. Amsterdam: John Benjamins.

Arnold, Jennifer. 2003. Multiple constraints on reference form. In John Du Bois, Lorraine Kumpf & William Ashby (eds.), *Preferred Argument Structure: Grammar as architecture for function*, 225–246. Amsterdam: John Benjamins.

Auer, Peter. 2005. Projection in interaction and projection in grammar. *Text* 25(1). 7–36.

Augsburger, Deborah. 2004. *Language socialization and shift in an Isthmus Zapotec community of Mexico.* University of Pennsylvannia dissertation.

Avelino, Heriberto. 2004. *Topics in Yalálag Zapotec, with particular reference to its phonetic structures.* University of California, Los Angeles dissertation.

Beam de Azcona, Rosemary. 2004. *A Coatlán-Loxicha Zapotec grammar.* University of California, Berkeley dissertation.

Benton, Joseph. 1987. Clause and sentence-level word order and discourse strategy in Chichicapan Zapotec oral narrative discourse. *SIL Mexico Workpapers* 9. 72–84.

Benton, Joseph. 1997. Aspect shift in Chichicapan Zapotec narrative discourse. *SIL Mexico Workpapers* 12. 34–46.

Bernini, Giuliano & Marcia Schwartz. 2006. *Pragmatic organization of discourse in the languages of Europe.* Berlin: Walter de Gruyter.

References

Black, Cheryl. 2000. *Quiegolani Zapotec syntax: A Principles and Parameters account*. Dallas: SIL International & The University of Texas at Arlington Publications in Linguistics.

Brickell, Timothy & Stephan Schnell. 2017. Do grammatical relations reflect information status? Reassessing Preferred Argument Structure theory against discourse data from Tondano. *Linguistic Typology* 21(1). 177–208.

Broadwell, George A. 1999. The interaction of focus and constituent order in San Dionicio Ocotepec Zapotec. In *Proceedings of the LFG 99 conference*.

Broadwell, George A. 2002. Preverbal positions and phrase boundaries in Zapotec. In *Annual meeting of the linguistic society of America*. San Francisco, CA.

Camacho, José, Rodrigo Gutiérrez-Bravo & Liliana Sánchez. 2010. *Information structure in indigenous languages of the Americas: Syntactic approaches*. Vol. 225. Berlin: Walter de Gruyter.

Campbell, Eric. 2011. Zenzontepec Chatino aspect morphology and Zapotecan verb classes. *International Journal of American Linguistics* 77(2). 219–246.

Campbell, Eric. 2017a. Otomanguean historical linguistics: Exploring the subgroups. *Language and Linguistics Compass* 11(7). e12244.

Campbell, Eric. 2017b. Otomanguean historical linguistics: Past, present, and prospects for the future. *Language and Linguistics Compass* 11(4). e12240.

Castillo Hernández, Carolina. 2014. Observaciones sobre la interfaz sintaxis-pragmática en narrativas de tres lenguas indígenas mexicanas. *Signo y Seña: Revista del Instituto de Lingüística* 25. 35–58.

Chafe, Wallace. 1976. Givenness, contrastiveness, definiteness, subjects, topics, and point of view. In Charles Li (ed.), *Subject and topic*, 27–55. New York: Academic Press.

Chafe, Wallace (ed.). 1980. *The pear stories: Cognitive, cultural, and linguistic aspects of narrative production*. Norwood: Ablex.

Chafe, Wallace. 1994. *Discourse, consciousness and time*. Chicago: University of Chicago Press.

Chávez Peón, Mario. 2010. *The interaction of metrical structure, tone, and phonation types in Quiaviní Zapotec*. University of British Columbia dissertation.

Crocco, Claudia. 2009. Topic accent and prosodic structure. In Lunella Mereu (ed.), *Information structure and its interfaces*, 15–49. Berlin: Mouton de Gruyter.

Dahlstrom, Amy. 1991. *Plains Cree morphosyntax*. New York: Garland.

Dahlstrom, Amy. 2003. Focus constructions in Meskwaki (Fox). In Miriam Butt & Tracy Holloway King (eds.), *The Proceedings of the LFG'03 Conference*, 144–163. Stanford: CSLI Publications.

Dahlstrom, Amy. 2014. Obviation and information structure in Meskwaki. In Monica Macaulay & Margaret Noodin (eds.), *Forty-sixth Algonquian Conference 2014*. Michigan State University Press.

Dixon, Robert M. W. 1979. Ergativity. *Language* 55(1). 59–138.

Downing, Pamela. 1980. Factors influencing lexical choice in narrative. In Wallace Chafe (ed.), *The Pear stories. Cognitive, cultural, and linguistic aspects of narrative production*, 89–126. Norwood: Ablex.

Dryer, Matthew. 2007. Word order. *Language typology and syntactic description* 1. 61–131.

Du Bois, John. 1987. The discourse basis of ergativity. *Language* 63(4). 805–855.

Du Bois, John. 2003a. Argument structure: Grammar in use. In John Du Bois, Lorraine Kumpf & William Ashby (eds.), *Preferred Argument Structure: Grammar as architecture for function*, 11–60. Philadelphia: John Benjamins.

Du Bois, John. 2003b. Discourse and grammar. In Michael Tomasello (ed.), *The new psychology of language: Cognitive and functional approaches to language structure*, vol. 2, 47–87. Mahwah, NJ: Lawrence Erlbaum.

Du Bois, John. 2006. The Pear Story in Sakapultek Maya: A case study of information flow and preferred argument structure. *Haciendo Lingüística: Homenaje a Paola Bentivoglio*. 191–222.

Du Bois, John, Lorraine Kumpf & William Ashby (eds.). 2003. *Preferred Argument Structure: Grammar as architecture for function*. Philadelphia: John Benjamins.

Du Bois, John, Stephan Schuetze-Coburn, Susanna Cummings & Danae Paolino. 1993. Outline of discourse transcription. In Jane Edwards & Martin Lampert (eds.), *Talking data: Transcription and coding in discourse research*, 45–89. Hillsdale, NJ: Erlbaum.

Enríquez Licón, Maniza. 2008. Clases verbales en zapoteco del Istmo. In Ausencia López Cruz & Michael Swanton (eds.), *Memorias del Coloquio María Teresa Fernández de Miranda*. Oaxaca, Mexico: Biblioteca Francisco de Burgoa.

Erteschik-Shir, Nomi. 2007. *Information structure: The syntax-discourse interface*. Oxford: Oxford University Press.

Everett, Caleb. 2009. A reconsideration of the motivations for preferred argument structure. *Studies in Language* 33(1). 1–24.

Fox, James. 1977. Roman Jakobson and the comparative study of parallelism. In James Fox, Daniel Armstrong & C. H. van Schooneveld (eds.), *Roman Jakobson: echoes of his scholarship*, 59–90. Lisse: Peter de Ridder Publishers.

Galant, Michael. 2006. *Comparative constructions in Spanish and San Lucas Quiaviní Zapotec*. Vol. 15. Münich: Lincom Europa.

References

Givón, Talmy (ed.). 1983. *Topic continuity in discourse: A quantitative cross-language study*. Amsterdam: Philadelphia: John Benjamins.

Gundel, Jeanette & Thorstein Fretheim. 2001. Topic and focus. In Laurence Horn & Gregory Ward (eds.), *Handbook of pragmatics*, 175–196. Oxford: Blackwell.

Gundel, Jeanette, Nancy Hedberg & Ron Zacharski. 1993. Cognitive status and the form of referring expressions in discourse. *Language* 69(2). 274–307.

Gundel, Jeannette, Mamadou Bassene, Bryan Gordon, Linda Humnick & Amel Khalfaoui. 2010. Testing predictions of the Givenness Hierarchy framework: A crosslinguistic investigation. *Journal of Pragmatics* 42(7). 1770–1785.

Haig, Geoffrey & Stefan Schnell. 2016. The discourse basis of ergativity revisited. *Language* 92(3). 591–618.

Haiman, John. 1978. Conditionals are topics. *Language* 54(3). 564–589.

Haspelmath, Martin. 2006. Preferred Argument Structure: Grammar as architecture for function (review). *Language* 83(4). 908–912.

Heath, Shirley B. 1972. *Telling tongues: Language policy in Mexico, colony to nation*. New York: Teachers College Press.

Heise, Jennifer. 2003. *Participant reference and tracking in San Francisco Ozolotepec Zapotec*. Graduate Institute of Applied Linguistics MA thesis.

Himmelmann, Nikolaus. 2006. Prosody in language documentation. In Jost Gippert, Nikolaus Himmelmann & Ulrike Mosel (eds.), *Essentials of language documentation*, 163–182. Berlin: Mouton de Gruyter.

Hopper, Paul & Sandra Thompson. 1980. Transitivity in grammar and discourse. *Language* 56(2). 251–299.

Jakobson, Roman. 1966. Grammatical parallelism and its Russian facet. *Language* 42(2). 399–429.

Kaufman, Terrence, John Justeson & Gabriela Pérez Báez. n.d. Lexical database of Sapoteko of Juchitán. Project for the Documentation of the Languages of Meso-America.

Kerslake, Celia. 1996. Future time reference in subordinate clauses in Turkish. In *Proceedings of the VIIIth International Conference on Turkish Linguistics*, 49–59.

König, Ekkehard & Peter Siemund. 2007. Speech act distinctions in grammar. In Timothy Shopen (ed.), *Language typology and syntactic description*, vol. 1, 276–324. Cambridge: Cambridge University Press.

Konnerth, Linda. 2013. Additive particle and discourse contrast marker: Evidence from Karbi (Tibeto-Burman) =ta. In *Information structure in spoken language corpora*. University of Bielefeld, Germany.

Kreikebaum, Wolfram. 1987. Fronting and related features in Santo Domingo Albarradas Zapotec. *SIL Mexico Workpapers* 9. 33–71.

Lambrecht, Knud. 1994. *Information structure and sentence form*. Cambridge: Cambridge University Press.

Lee, Felicia. 2000. VP remnant movement and VSO in Quiavini Zapotec. In Andrew Carnie & Eithne Guilfoyle (eds.), *The syntax of verb-initial languages*, 143–162. New York: Oxford University Press.

Li, Charles & Sandra Thompson. 1976. Subject and topic: A new typology of language. In Charles Li (ed.), *Subject and topic*, 459–489. New York: Academic Press.

Lillehaugen, Brook. 2006. *Expressing location in Tlacolula Valley Zapotec*. University of California, Los Angeles dissertation.

Lillehaugen, Brook. 2008. El morfema *làa'* y su uso en el zapoteco de Tlacolula de Matamoros. In *X Encuentro Internacional de Lingüística en el noroeste*. Hermosillo, Sonora, Mexico.

Lillehaugen, Brook. 2016. The syntax of preverbal subjects in Colonial Valley Zapotec. In *VII Syntax of the World's Languages International Conference and Workshop*. Mexico City, Mexico.

Long, Rebecca. 1985. Topicalization in Zoogocho Zapotec expository discourse. *SIL Mexico Workpapers* 7. 61–100.

MacLaury, Robert. 1989. Zapotec body-part locatives: Prototypes and metaphoric extensions. *International Journal of American Linguistics* 55(2). 119–154.

Marchese, Lynell. 1977. Subordinate clauses as topics in Godié. *Studies in African Linguistics, Supplement* 7. 157–164.

Marchese, Lynell. 1987. On the role of conditionals in Godié procedural discourse. In *Coherence and grounding in discourse: Outcome of a symposium, Eugene, Oregon*, vol. 11. Amsterdam: John Benjamins Publishing.

Marlett, Stephen & Velma Pickett. 1987. The syllable structure and aspect morphology of Isthmus Zapotec. *International Journal of American Linguistics* 53(4). 398–422.

Marlett, Stephen & Velma Pickett. 1996. El pronombre inaudible en el zapoteco del Istmo. *III Encuentro de Lingüística en el Noroeste*. 119–150.

Matić, Dejan & Daniel Wedgwood. 2013. The meanings of focus: The significance of an interpretation-based category in cross-linguistic analysis. *Journal of Linguistics* 49(1). 127–163.

McComsey, Melanie. 2015. *Bilingual spaces: Approaches to linguistic relativity in bilingual Mexico*. University of California, San Diego dissertation.

Mereu, Lunella (ed.). 2009. *Information structure and its interfaces*. Berlin: Mouton de Gruyter.

Mithun, Marianne. 1992. Is basic word order universal. In Doris Payne (ed.), *Pragmatics of word order flexibility*, 15–61. Philadelphia: John Benjamins.

Mithun, Marianne. 1995. Morphological and prosodic forces shaping word order. In Pamela Downing & Michael Noonan (eds.), *Word order in discourse*, 387–423. Philadelphia: John Benjamins.

Mock, Carol. 1983. Tone sandhi in Isthmus Zapotec: An autosegmental account. *Linguistic Analysis* 12(1). 91–139.

Mock, Carol. 1985a. A systemic phonology of Isthmus Zapotec prosodies. In James Benson & William Greaves (eds.), *Systemic perspectives on discourse: Selected theoretical papers from the Ninth International Systemic Workshop*, 349–372. Norwood: Ablex.

Mock, Carol. 1985b. Relations between pitch accent and stress. In *Papers from the General Session at the Twenty-First Regional Meeting of the Chicago Linguistic Society*, 256–274.

Mock, Carol. 1988. Pitch accent and stress in Isthmus Zapotec. In Harry van der Hulst (ed.), *Autosegmental studies on pitch accent*, 197–223. Dordrecht: Foris.

Mock, Carol. 1990. Temporal orientation without tenses: The deixis of time in Isthmus Zapotec. In Garza Cuarón, Beatriz and Levy, Paulette (ed.), *Homenaje a Jorge A. Suárez: Lingüística indoamericana e hispánica*, 367–379. Colégio de México.

Opengin, Ergin. 2013. Topicalisation in Central Kurdish: Additive particle and other means. In *Information structure in spoken language corpora*. University of Bielefeld, Germany.

Ozerov, Pavel. 2015. Information structure without topic and focus: Differential Object Marking in Burmese. *Studies in Language* 39(2). 386–423.

Paul, Lewis, Gary Simons & Charles Fennig (eds.). 2016. *Ethnologue: Languages of the world*. 19th. Dallas: SIL International. http://www.ethnologue.com.

Payne, Doris. 1990. *The pragmatics of word order: Typological dimensions of verb initial languages*. Berlin: Walter de Gruyter.

Payne, Doris. 1995. Verb initial languages and information order. In Pamela Downing & Michael Noonan (eds.), *Word order in discourse*, 449–85. Philadelphia: John Benjamins.

Pekarek Doehler, Simona. 2011. Emergent grammar for all practical purposes: The on-line formatting of left and right dislocations in French conversation. In Peter Auer & Stefan Pfänder (eds.), *Constructions: Emerging and Emergent*, 45–87. Berlin: Walter de Gruyter.

Pérez Báez, Gabriela. 2011. Spatial frames of reference preferences in Juchitán Zapotec. *Language Sciences* 33(6). 943–960.

Pérez Báez, Gabriela. 2015. Morphological valence-changing processes in Juchitán Zapotec. In Natalie Operstein & Aaron Huey Sonnenschein (eds.), *Valence changes in zapotec: synchrony, diachrony, typology*, vol. 110 (Typological Studies in Language), 93–116. John Benjamins Publishing Company.

Persons, David. 1979. Plot structure in Lachixio Zapotec discourse. In Linda Jones & Robert Longacre (eds.), *Discourse studies in Mesoamerican languages*, vol. 1, 123–40. Dallas: Summer Institute of Linguistics.

Pickett, Velma. 1960. The grammatical hierarchy of Isthmus Zapotec. *Language* 36(1). 3–101.

Pickett, Velma. 1979. *Vocabulario zapoteco del Istmo.* Mexico: Summer Institute of Linguistics.

Pickett, Velma, Cheryl Black & Vicente Marcial Cerqueda. 1998. *Gramática popular del zapoteco del Istmo.* Oaxaca: Centro de Investigación y Desarrollo Binnizá; Instituto Lingüístico de Verano.

Piper, Michael. 1995. The functions of 'lëë' in Xanica Zapotec narrative discourse with some implications for comparative Zapotec. *SIL Mexico Workpapers* 11. 67–78.

Prince, Ellen. 1981. Toward a taxonomy of given-new information. In Peter Cole (ed.), *Radical pragmatics*, 223–255. New York: Academic Press.

Rendón, Juan José. 1995. *Diversificación de las lenguas zapotecas.* Oaxaca, Mexico: Instituto Oaxaqueño de las Culturas, Centro de Investigaciones y Estudios Superiores de Antropología Social.

Riggs, David. 1987. Paragraph analysis for Amatlán Zapotec. *SIL Mexico Workpapers* 9. 1–11.

Riggs, David & Stephen Marlett. 2010. The *le'e* focus phrase: Structural aspects. In Cheryl Black, H. Andrew Black & Stephen Marlett (eds.), *The Zapotec grammar files.* Summer Institute of Linguistics.

Sacks, Harvey, Emanuel A. Schegloff & Gail Jefferson. 1974. A simplest systematics for the organization of turn-taking for conversation. *Language* 50(4). 696–735.

Saynes-Vásquez, Edaena. 2002. *Zapotec language shift and reversal in Juchitán, Mexico.* University of Arizona dissertation.

Scarano, Antonietta. 2009. A the prosodic annotation of C-ORAL-ROM and the structure of information in spoken language. In Lunella Mereu (ed.), *Information structures and its interfaces*, 51–74. Berlin & New York: Mouton de Gruyter.

Sherzer, Joel. 1987. A discourse-centered approach to language and culture. *American Anthropologist* 89(2). 295–309.

Sicoli, Mark. 2007. *Tono: A linguistic ethnography of tone and voice in a Zapotec region (Mexico)*. University of Michigan dissertation.

Sicoli, Mark. 2010. Shifting voices with participant roles: Voice qualities and speech registers in Mesoamerica. *Language in Society* 39(4). 521–553.

Sicoli, Mark. 2015. Agency and verb valence in Lachixío Zapotec. In Natalie Operstein & Aaron Huey Sonnenschein (eds.), *Valence changes in Zapotec: synchrony, diachrony, typology*, vol. 110 (Typological Studies in Language), 191–212. John Benjamins Publishing Company.

Silverstein, Michael. 1976. Hierarchy of features and ergativity. In R. M. W. Dixon (ed.), *Grammatical categories in Australian languages*, 112–171. Canberra: Australian Institute of Aboriginal Studies.

Silverstein, Michael. 1984. On the pragmatic 'poetry' of prose: Parallelism, repetition, and cohesive structure in the time course of dyadic conversation. In Deborah Schiffrin (ed.), *Meaning, form, and use in context: Linguistic applications*, 181–199. Washington: Georgetown University Press.

Smith-Stark, Thomas. 2002. Las clases verbales del zapoteco de chichicapan. In Zarina Estrada Fernández & Rosa María Ortiz Ciscomani (eds.), *Proceedings of the VI Encuentro Internacional de Lingüística en el Noroeste*. Sonora, Mexico: Editorial Universidad de Sonora.

Smith-Stark, Thomas. 2003. Algunas isoglosas zapotecas. In *Proceedings of the III Coloquio de Mauricio Swadesh*. Mexico City: UNAM: Instituto de Investigaciones Antropológicas.

Sonnenschein, Aaron H. 2005. *A descriptive grammar of San Bartolomé Zoogocho Zapotec*. Munich: Lincom Europa.

Suárez, Jorge. 1983. *The Mesoamerican Indian languages*. Cambridge: Cambridge University Press.

Swadesh, Maurice. 1947. The phonemic structure of Proto-Zapotec. *International Journal of American Linguistics* 13(4). 220–230.

Thompson, Sandra, Robert Longacre & Shinja Hwang. 2007. Adverbial clauses. In Timothy Shopen (ed.), *Language typology and syntactic description*, vol. 2, 237–300. Cambridge: Cambridge University Press.

Toledo Bustamante, Nadxieli. 2018. *Socialization patterns, emerging attention, and language choice in Juchitán, Oaxaca, Mexico*. University of Chicago dissertation.

Van Valin, Robert. 1999. A typology of the interaction of focus structure and syntax. In Ekatarina Raxilina & Yakov Testelec (eds.), *Typology and the theory of language: From description to explanation*, 511–524. Moscow: Languages of Russian Culture.

Ward, Michael. 1987. A focus particle in Quioquitani Zapotec. *SIL Mexico Work-papers* 9. 26–32.

Yip, Moira. 2002. *Tone.* Cambridge: Cambridge University Press.

Zhang, Jie. 2002. *The effects of duration and sonority on contour tone distribution: A typological survey and formal analysis.* New York: Routledge.

Zoll, Cheryl. 2003. Optimal tone mapping. *Linguistic Inquiry* 34(2). 225–268.

Name index

Arellanes, Francisco, 13, 20
Ariel, Mira, 49–51, 65–67, 69, 72, 73, 128
Arnold, Jennifer, 52, 56–58
Auer, Peter, 123
Augsburger, Deborah, 5, 6
Avelino, Heriberto, 1, 20

Beam de Azcona, Rosemary, 1, 25
Benton, Joseph, 7
Bernini, Giuliano, 1
Black, Cheryl, 36
Brickell, Timothy, 44, 49, 67
Broadwell, George A., 36, 87

Camacho, José, 1
Campbell, Eric, 1, 23
Castillo Hernández, Carolina, 1
Chafe, Wallace, 2, 20, 21, 41, 42, 69, 120
Chávez Peón, Mario, 13, 20
Crocco, Claudia, 109

Dahlstrom, Amy, 85
Dixon, Robert M. W., 44
Downing, Pamela, 67
Dryer, Matthew, 23, 25–27
Du Bois, John, 20, 41, 43–45, 47, 48, 50, 54, 56, 64, 66, 73, 128

Enríquez Licón, Maniza, 23
Erteschik-Shir, Nomi, 1
Everett, Caleb, 48, 49, 52, 67

Fox, James, 104
Fretheim, Thorstein, 69

Galant, Michael, 29
Givón, Talmy, 67, 68
Gundel, Jeanette, 69, 70, 72, 73, 126, 129
Gundel, Jeannette, 71

Haig, Geoffrey, 44, 49, 67
Haiman, John, 29, 120, 123
Haspelmath, Martin, 48, 49, 52, 67
Heath, Shirley B., 5
Heise, Jennifer, 7
Himmelmann, Nikolaus, 8
Hopper, Paul, 58

Jakobson, Roman, 104

Kaufman, Terrence, 7
Kerslake, Celia, 120
König, Ekkehard, 123
Konnerth, Linda, 120
Kreikebaum, Wolfram, 7

Lambrecht, Knud, 2, 11, 38, 54, 72, 87, 88, 92, 93, 97, 100, 109, 110, 120, 125, 129
Lee, Felicia, 25, 36, 87
Li, Charles, 120
Lillehaugen, Brook, 1, 19
Long, Rebecca, 7

MacLaury, Robert, 19, 26

Marchese, Lynell, 120
Marlett, Stephen, 6, 7, 23, 62, 77
Matić, Dejan, 121, 131
McComsey, Melanie, 6
Mereu, Lunella, 1
Mithun, Marianne, 51, 72, 101
Mock, Carol, 6, 20, 24

Opengin, Ergin, 120
Ozerov, Pavel, 131

Paul, Lewis, 5
Payne, Doris, 25, 29, 35, 36, 123
Pekarek Doehler, Simona, 123
Pérez Báez, Gabriela, 23, 24, 26
Persons, David, 7
Pickett, Velma, 6, 13, 16, 23–25, 37, 62,
        77, 96, 97, 119
Piper, Michael, 7
Prince, Ellen, 69

Rendón, Juan José, 4
Riggs, David, 7

Sacks, Harvey, 123
Saynes-Vásquez, Edaena, 6
Scarano, Antonietta, 9
Schnell, Stefan, 44, 49, 67
Schnell, Stephan, 44, 49, 67
Schwartz, Marcia, 1
Sherzer, Joel, 8
Sicoli, Mark, 7, 19, 24, 25, 121
Siemund, Peter, 123
Silverstein, Michael, 57, 105
Smith-Stark, Thomas, 1, 23
Sonnenschein, Aaron H., 1, 25
Suárez, Jorge, 24
Swadesh, Maurice, 13

Thompson, Sandra, 58, 120, 122, 123

Toledo Bustamante, Nadxieli, 6

Van Valin, Robert, 11, 88, 100, 101, 108

Ward, Michael, 7
Wedgwood, Daniel, 121, 131

Yip, Moira, 18

Zhang, Jie, 18
Zoll, Cheryl, 18

Language index

Achenese, 44
Algonquian, 85

Brazilian Portuguese, 44, 45[4]

Cayuga, 101
Coatlán-Loxicha Zapotec, 25[10]

English, 9, 44, 45, 45[4], 48, 88, 89, 92, 94, 100–102

Finnish, 44
French, 44, 45, 88, 89, 92, 94, 100–102

Hebrew, 44, 45, 45[4]

Japanese, 44, 45, 88, 89, 92, 94

Karbi, 120

Lachixío Zapotec, 19, 24[9], 25[10]
Lisu, 120

Mapudungun, 44

Nepali, 44

Papago, 44, 45

Russian, 101, 102, 108

Sakapultek Maya, 43, 47
San Bartolomé Zoogocho Zapotec, 25[10]
San Lucas Quiavini Zapotec, 25[10]

Somali, 121[5]
Spanish, ix, 1, 4–7, 9, 26, 27, 29, 30, 41, 44, 45, 91

Turkish, 120

Subject index

accessibility, 2, 49–51, 51[8], 52, 54, 55, 55[10], 56–60, 63, 65–69, 71–73, 85, 87, 110, 125, 128, 129

adverbial, 11, 27, 29, 30, 33, 34, 36, 39, 78, 105, 118, 120, 122, 124

animacy, 48, 49, 52, 54, 55, 57, 67, 111

argument focus, 3, 11, 38, 88, 92–94, 96–100, 103–105, 107, 108, 112, 128, 130

broad focus, 88, 93, 102, 108

chiastic structure, 3, 105, 107, 108

cognitive staging area, 69, 73, 128

conditional construction, 123

constituent order, 2, 3, 10, 22, 23, 25, 26, 33–35, 39, 87, 100, 101, 115, 118, 125, 129, 130

contrastive topic, 131

demonstrative, vii, 55, 56, 71

dependent pronoun, 37, 61, 64[13], 97

discourse particle, vii, 2, 3, 38, 109, 123, 131

flexible syntax, 87

floating tone, 90

focal stress, 88, 89, 91, 92, 94, 100, 101

focus, 2–4, 7, 11, 19–23, 36, 39–41, 43, 52, 61, 69–71, 71[16], 72, 73, 85[3], 87, 88, 88[1], 89[2], 92[3], 93[4], 96, 98, 100–103, 107, 109, 110, 118, 125, 128, 130, 131

focus domain, 88, 89, 91–94, 100, 102, 103, 107, 108, 110–112, 115, 126, 127, 130

focus structure, 85, 87, 88, 100–102, 108, 130

givenness hierarchy, 109

glottalization, 9, 16, 17

grammatical role, 3, 47, 51, 52, 55, 55[10], 56, 57, 59, 62, 68, 72, 73, 128

identificational construction, 112, 113, 115, 116

independent pronoun, 64, 64[13], 75, 97, 121, 124

information pressure, 47

information structure, 1, 2, 4, 7, 8, 10, 11, 13, 16, 22, 23, 36, 39–41, 87, 100, 101, 107, 110, 126–131

intonation, 2, 3, 7, 8, 19, 20, 38, 43, 51[8], 72, 90, 100, 105, 107, 108, 118, 121, 123, 125, 130

intonation unit, 3, 20, 42, 43, 43[2], 64, 64[14], 65, 87, 90, 93, 95, 100, 102, 103[5], 105, 107, 108, 117, 118, 121

Juchitán, v, vi, 1, 4, 5, 6[2], 7

laryngealization, 15–17

marked topic, 64, 64[14], 110, 126, 129

narrow focus, 88, 93, 102, 108
nominal expression, 39, 50, 70–73, 128

pitch accent, 22, 72, 89, 91–93, 95, 102, 104
potential focus domain, 101, 102, 108
pragmatic status, 3, 69, 71–73, 85, 129
predicate focus, 3, 11, 88, 89, 91–93, 96, 97, 100, 102–108, 128, 130
Preferred Argument Structure, 10, 41, 43, 69, 73, 128
presupposition, 38, 88, 94–96, 103, 116
prosody, 3, 7, 8, 9[3], 10, 16, 18, 19, 22, 39, 40, 109

question particle, vii, 27, 31[12], 34

recency, 52, 55, 57–60, 63, 67

salience, 3, 11, 50–52, 56–58, 60, 63, 65, 85, 129
sentence focus, 3, 11, 53, 88, 92, 93, 100, 107, 110[2]
subordinate clause, 27, 30, 34

third person, vii, 3, 10, 43, 52, 61, 64, 65, 81, 82, 84, 85, 117, 124, 125, 129, 131
third person enclitic, 90, 99, 117
third person form, 79, 81, 82, 117
third person pronoun, vi, 60, 62
tonal system, 3, 13, 16, 22
tone, ix, 2, 3, 7–9, 15–18, 18[3], 19, 20, 22, 39, 90, 91, 96, 118, 122
topic, 2–4, 7, 11, 22, 23, 29, 36, 39–41, 47, 63, 64[14], 68, 70, 81, 85,

85[3], 87–89, 91, 92, 99, 100, 103, 103[5], 109, 109[1], 110–118, 120–122, 125, 126, 128–130, 130[1], 131
topic continuity, 51, 55, 72, 73
topic marker, 40, 64[14], 118, 120, 122
topic promotion, 68, 103[5], 125, 126, 130[1]
topic-comment, 11, 88[1], 104, 111, 115, 126, 129, 130
topic-comment construction, 88, 111, 112, 117
topicalization, 96, 103[5], 111
topicalization construction, 115–118, 126, 130[1]
typology of focus structure, 11, 88, 100, 108

verb-initial construction, 89, 93, 108, 111, 112
verb-initial language, 1, 2, 11, 35, 87
verb-initial syntax, 2, 7, 10, 39, 130
vowel phonation, 20, 22, 38

zero form, 3, 10, 61–63, 75–79, 81, 82, 84, 85, 116[3], 129

www.ingramcontent.com/pod-product-compliance
Lightning Source LLC
Chambersburg PA
CBHW080914100426
42812CB00007B/2274